OXFORD*Playscripts*

Series editors: Steve Barlow and Steve Skidmore

Geoffrey Chaucer   *adapted by Martin Riley*

The Canterbury Tales

Oxford University Press

Oxford University Press, Great Clarendon Street, Oxford OX2 6DP

Oxford   New York
Athens   Auckland   Bangkok   Bogotá   Buenos Aires
Calcutta   Cape Town   Chennai   Dar es Salaam   Delhi
Florence   Hong Kong   Istanbul   Karachi   Kuala Lumpur
Madrid   Melbourne   Mexico City   Mumbai   Nairobi   Paris
São Paulo   Singapore   Taipei   Tokyo   Toronto   Warsaw

and associated companies in
Berlin   Ibadan

Oxford is a trade mark of Oxford University Press

This adaptation of *The Canterbury Tales* © Martin Riley 1998
Activity section © Steve Barlow and Steve Skidmore 1998
First published 1998
Reprinted 1998

ISBN 0 19 831293 8

Printed and bound in Great Britain at Cambridge University Press

The publishers would like to thank the following for permission
to reproduce photographs:

The Dean and Chapter, Canterbury Cathedral: p 109;
The Witt Library, Courtauld Institute of Art: p 104;
Mary Evans Picture Library: pp 19, 41, 53, 76, 83;
Getty Images/Hulton Picture Library: p 101.

Illustrations are by Julian Page

Cover illustration by Simon Fell

Thanks to John Mee and Alive and Kicking Theatre Company,
Leeds for their contribution – especially to the composer, Jack
Glover, the designer, Julie Robinson, and above all the actors whose
talent has helped shape and hone this latest version of 'the work':
Richard Parry, Pat George, Donna Smith, Gareth Harwood,
Johnny Hoskins, Mike Rogers, Amanda Kernot, and Joanna Swain.

Contents

	Page
The Characters	4
A Note on the Set	6
Acting Styles	8
The Play: The Canterbury Tales	10
Introduction	10
The Pardoner's Tale	18
Interlude	39
The Nun's Priest's Tale	41
Interlude	51
The Wife of Bath's Tale (Part One)	52
Introduction to Part Two	61
The Wife of Bath's Tale (Part Two)	62
Interlude	75
The Knight's Tale	76
Interlude	82
The Miller's Tale	84
Finale	98
Activities	100
About the Author	101
Chaucer's World	102
Chaucer's Pilgrims	104
Chaucer's Language	107
What the Adapter Says	110
Design Ideas	111

4

Characters

In order of their
appearance on stage:

Jocasta Michelangelo Giovanni Amelia	*four eternally young medieval Alchemists who once stumbled on the secret of eternal life; the high energy, circus-style presenters of the tales*
Geoffrey Chaucer	*author of The Canterbury Tales, suspended in a strange comatose state between this world and the next; played until the last scene by a mannequin (or a very still person)*
The Pardoner	*a medieval seller of holy relics and pardons; a cross between a tricksy street trader and a 'hell-fire and damnation' American TV evangelist*
Tom	*a medieval hooligan; young, keen and desperate to be one of the lads*
Dick	*a medieval hooligan; mad, bad and dangerous*
Harry	*a medieval hooligan; a manic joker who thinks he's hilarious*
Ambrosius	*a medieval hooligan; the super-cool leader of the gang; chosen from the audience*
Old Man	*wearing a blanket as a cloak and walking with a stick*
The Nun's Priest	*a gentle old soul, but an enthusiastic teller of tales*
Chaunticleer	*a noble, proud and handsome singing cock; he fancies himself*
Voice 1 Voice 2	*shouts from off stage*
Pertelote	*Chaunticleer's favourite hen; all fuss and bustle; she can be prim and proper, but also saucy and romantic*
Sir Russell Fox	*a sly and crafty fox; talks like a gentleman but barks like a beast*
The Wife of Bath	*a straight talking woman of experience; has been married five times; she enjoys men and money and likes to be boss*

Sir Codsbrain	*a macho knight at the court of King Arthur who thinks he's God's gift to women*
Squire	*to Sir Codsbrain (non-speaking)*
Amanda the maiden	*a beautiful young girl; inexperienced but with plenty of attitude*
Queen Guinevere	*a woman in the prime of middle age; tally-ho, jolly hockey sticks and very assertive*
King Arthur	*a hopeless, old, upper-crust, forgetful dodderer*
Old Woman	*a mysterious, ugly and ragged crone*
Priest	*a suitable person chosen from the audience*
The Knight	*an old soldier and plain-speaking man of action*
Theseus	*the Duke of Athens; a nobleman with the voice of authority*
Emily	*Theseus's sister-in-law; a beautiful young woman who knows her own mind but keeps getting it made up for her by men*
Palamon	*a defeated young enemy knight languishing in an Athens prison; he is smitten with love for Emily*
Arcite	*another imprisoned young knight who also falls in love with Emily*
Venus	*the goddess of love*
Mars	*the god of war*
Diana	*goddess of the hunt; free and strong*
The Miller	*a lying, cheating, argumentative, foul-mouthed drunk*
Alison	*a passionate, wild-spirited girl who has been married off to John*
John	*a rich, miserly, boring old carpenter*
Nicholas	*John's lodger; a crafty, young art student, in love with Alison*
Absolon	*a cute, sweet-faced, tousle-haired young man, also in love with Alison; he helps out at church*
Gervais	*a blacksmith; big and burly*

A Note on the Set

The Stage
The show is designed to be played end on or with a thrust.
There should be a 'street theatre' feel about the set and no
pretence other than that the audience is to be entertained on
the stage by players and storytellers.

Upstage is a large, simple, raised booth or cart with curtains
which can be opened and closed on three sides. This is just
one acting area. (For classroom/drama studio purposes, the
booth may be made of rostra.) Canvas cloths can be hung
at the back of the booth and stage left and right to provide
changes of scenery. Steps provide access to the back of the
booth, allowing players to appear in the booth unseen.

There are also acting areas left, right and downstage of
the booth. A floor cloth, perhaps with a non-naturalistic
alchemical design may be used to define the acting area in
front of the booth. Downstage left and right are two open
frame pulpits which provide bases for the story-telling.
Downstage far right is a free standing coatstand where
costumes can be hung for use during the show. Players who
are not directly involved in the action can sit around the edges
of the stage joining in where appropriate, and encouraging the
audience to respond to the events taking place on the stage.

The set also contains a big trestle table (or rostrum block),
two solid benches and a set of steps. The table is movable but
strong enough and big enough for three people to stand on it
together. These items can be shifted into new positions as
required during the play. (See diagrams in playscript.)

Music and Sound Effects
The music from the original production is available for the
songs, etc., but students should feel free to compose their own.
All sound effects should be simple and as 'live' as possible as
in a medieval mystery play. Taped sound effects would be out
of place, but noises made with improvised percussion
instruments would be fine. Musical instruments, percussion
and 'junk' percussion should not be hidden from view. They
can be hung on, or fixed to the frames of the two pulpits for
the storytellers to use. A 'story bell' completes the collection.

This is rung by each pilgrim to indicate the start of his or her tale. Other musical and percussion instruments can be played, as appropriate, by other members of the cast.

The Stand-Up Bed

The stand-up bed is used in The Miller's Tale. It is created by hanging two pieces of material (which become bedcovers) inside the booth. The actors then stand between the covers as if they are in a vertical bed, facing the audience. (See below.)

Illustrations

The illustrations of the pilgrims within the playscript are taken from the margins of the Ellesmere manuscript, illuminated within a few years of Chaucer's death.

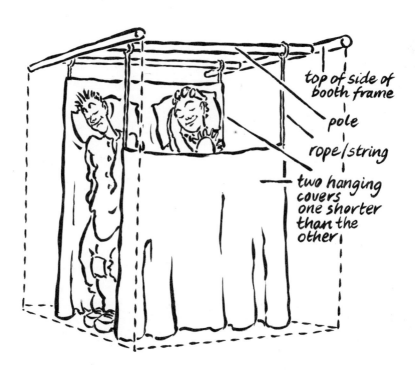

Acting Styles

Before you read this play, it is important to understand
something about the acting styles needed to perform it
effectively.

The Alchemists
The tales are introduced by four Alchemists: Jocasta,
Michelangelo, Giovanni, and Amelia. Alchemists were the
scientists of their time. They spent their lives trying to discover
great secrets, such as how to turn lead into gold, or as in this
play, the 'secret of eternal youth'. In **The Canterbury Tales**,
the Alchemists act like TV game show hosts; they talk directly
to the audience, tell jokes, introduce the characters, and help
the audience understand what is going on.

Audience Participation
In this play, members of the audience are occasionally chosen
to get up and join in with the action. Of course, the actors
can never know exactly what the person they choose to be
Ambrosius (in The Pardoner's Tale) or the priest (in The
Wife of Bath's Tale) is going to do, so no two performances
will ever be the same. These moments need a great deal of
careful rehearsal so that the actors are working 'on the same
wavelength' and are confident enough in their roles to cope
with the unexpected.

Commedia dell'Arte
The knockabout acting style of this playscript is based on a
style of theatre which began in Italy during the Sixteenth
century. In Commedia dell'Arte the dialogue was improvised;
the actors wore masks so that the audience could immediately
recognize their favourite characters; and the story was usually
very simple. The plays were often put on by travelling
companies which would set up and perform anywhere they
thought they could attract an audience.

There was lots of audience participation, and the plays were
comic and often very rude! The actors also used mime,
juggling and acrobatics to keep the action non-stop. One
character, Pulcinella, reached the English theatre and became

Mr Punch of the Punch and Judy show. A type of Commedia style is still enjoyed today by actors and audiences at traditional Christmas Pantomimes.

This adaptation of **The Canterbury Tales** is written to be performed in the Commedia style. The performers would benefit from some training in mime, and story-telling, and Commedia dell'Arte techniques before rehearsing with the script.

Mummers' Plays

Mumming is a very simple, traditional form of English theatre. It has been performed ever since the early Thirteenth century. Most of the plays are about the same group of characters. There is a hero, usually St George, who is challenged to a fight by a Saracen. The Saracen is killed, but then brought back to life by a Doctor.

Mummers' plays were performed in the street, the market and the tavern. There was no stage; the characters would simply stride forward and introduce themselves, and the play would begin. The actors used loud voices, big gestures and lots of energy. (Shakespeare makes fun of this sort of acting in *A Midsummer Night's Dream*.) This is the style in which the story of Palamon and Arcite in The Knight's Tale should be performed.

You may also find it helpful to read Martin Riley's What the Adapter Says on page 110.

Introduction

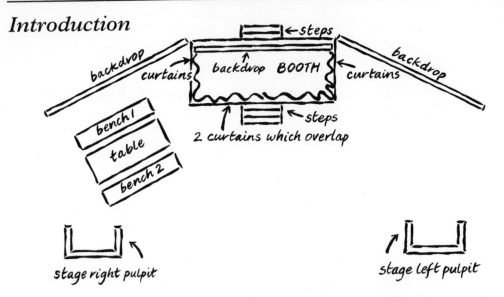

The stage is set with the steps placed centre front of the booth. Stage right is a trestle table with a bench either side of the table's longest side.

The stage manager gives a loud whistle to start the show. This whistle is answered by lots of enthusiastic whistles, shouts, and noises from backstage. **Jocasta** and **Michelangelo** bound instantly on stage in carnival mood and greet the audience with plenty of pace, excitement and physical energy.

Michelangelo	Caramba la mamba!
Jocasta	Holta la volta!
Michelangelo	Mango la tango!
Jocasta	Twista la vista!
Michelangelo	Ola!
Jocasta	Olé!!
Michelangelo	Olo!!!

Jocasta	(*Suddenly putting on the voice of an over-sincere TV presenter*) Hello.
Michelangelo	(*Like an even more sincere TV presenter*) Hi.
Jocasta	(*Changing back to circus-style and introducing Michelangelo to the audience*) Michelangelo!

There is applause. **Michelangelo** *bows.*

Michelangelo	(*Introducing Jocasta to the audience*) Jocasta!

There is more applause. **Jocasta** *bows.*

Michelangelo	(*Passionately, with a flourish*) Oh lovely audience, we love you so much – we lay our feet at your hearts!
Jocasta	(*More passionately, hugging herself*) You are so lovely – we wish we could embarrass you all!
Michelangelo	Ladies and gentlemen, boys and girls.
Jocasta	Grandmas and grandads.
Michelangelo	Little tiny babies.

Any special welcomes may be improvised here along the lines of the two below.

Jocasta	All you Barnsley FC supporters!
Michelangelo	You lot with the nose rings in the back row!
Jocasta	Hello everyone and welcome to…
Michelangelo	…the long playing…
Jocasta	…chart busting…
Michelangelo	…medieval…
Jocasta	…smash hit of the millennium…

Jocasta Michelangelo	(*Triumphantly*) The Canterbury Tales!
Michelangelo	(*Proudly*) With the original, award-winning cast!
Jocasta	Yes, Michelangelo here is six hundred and sixteen years old! You wouldn't guess to look at him would you? Well, maybe.
Michelangelo	(*Trying to get his own back*) And Jocasta here …is exactly the same age as me.
Jocasta	I'm twenty-two! And I've been twenty-two since 1400 AD, since the day we discovered the secret…
Jocasta Michelangelo	(*Hushed and intense*) The secret of eternal life!
	*Jocasta and **Michelangelo** snap into a dramatic TV documentary style and move smartly downstage to opposite sides.*
Jocasta	Thursday, October the twenty-fifth, 1400 AD.
Michelangelo	The day they say that Geoffrey Chaucer died. The date on his tomb in Westminster Abbey.
Jocasta	But Chaucer didn't die!
Michelangelo	Oh no!
Jocasta	Not quite. We found him just in time.
	***Michelangelo** and **Jocasta** suddenly switch into showbiz style, singing and dancing downstage centre.*
Jocasta Michelangelo	Just in time, we found him just in time!
	They switch again into a lively TV chat-show style.
Jocasta	Ladies and gentlemen, Geoffrey Chaucer isn't buried in Poets' Corner in Westminster Abbey.

Michelangelo	Oh no – he's here with us tonight!
Jocasta	Let's give him a big round of applause!
Michelangelo	The author of The Canterbury Tales.
Jocasta **Michelangelo** }	Geoffrey Chaucer!

Jocasta leads the audience and the rest of the cast in a football chant.

Jocasta	Geoff-er-ee! Geoff-er-ee! Geoff-er-ee!

This does not last long and the audience are not allowed to get carried away. The cast turn the chant of 'Geoff-er-ee!' into a churchy plainchant. **Giovanni** *and* **Amelia** *enter through the audience. They are carrying Geoffrey Chaucer, who is covered with a shroud. This is done in an over-solemn way to make it funny.* **Giovanni** *and* **Amelia** *place Geoffrey respectfully on the stage. All the cast continue chanting, putting their hands together in prayer, and lifting their eyes to heaven as if in a trance.*

Cast	Geoff-or-y. Geoff-or-y. Ge-e-e-eoff-or-y.
Alchemists	Famous for his po-o-o-etry.
Giovanni **Amelia** }	Especially his tales of Canter-bury.
Jocasta **Michelangelo** }	His name forever lives in his-tor-y.
Giovanni **Amelia** }	And though it seems most u-u-un-likely.
Alchemists	His body also lives immortally.
Cast	(*Echoing*) His body also lives immortally.

*The **Alchemists** catch each other's eyes, and suddenly break from their trance. The chanting stops. Ignoring Geoffrey, the **Alchemists** greet each other in a wild circus-style, leaping around, slapping hands, swinging, and hugging each other.*

Giovanni   Michelangelo!

Michelangelo   Giovanni!

Amelia   Jocasta!

Jocasta   Amelia!

In the crazy confusion someone accidentally bumps into Geoffrey.

Amelia   (*Immediately concerned*) Geoffrey!

*The **Alchemists** crowd round. There is no movement from Geoffrey. The **Alchemists** explain to the audience.*

Amelia   Geoffrey isn't quite dead.

Giovanni   He isn't quite alive either!

*The **Alchemists** move downstage of Geoffrey. They tell their story, with mime, to the audience.*

Amelia   It was two o'clock in the afternoon, Wednesday, October the twenty-fifth, 1400.

***Jocasta** and **Michelangelo** kneel facing each other and make a cauldron with their arms. **Amelia** and **Giovanni** stir it with a giant imaginary ladle.*

Amelia   We were mixing up a cure for the Black Death!

Alchemists   A cure for the Black Death!

Giovanni	It worked!
Amelia	(*Walking away from the 'cauldron'*) Certainly it worked! How many people here today have the Black Death?

*The **Alchemists** look around the audience for plague victims.*

Michelangelo	(*Pointing at audience members*) One, two, three, four...
Giovanni	(*Interrupting*) I remember it well. It was a Friday afternoon...
Amelia	Wednesday!
Jocasta **Michelangelo** }	Saturday!

*   **Giovanni** continues the mime.*

Giovanni	It was Thursday morning – and we were pouring the waste slops from our experiments into a bowl on the floor.

*   **Amelia** turns into a dog as she speaks and acts out the story.*

Amelia	The mangy flea bitten old dog from next door crept in and started licking it up. (*Reacting as if she's had an electric shock*) Zing!

*   **Amelia** leaps about the stage, full of energy, like a dog in a TV dog food commercial.*

Amelia	Woof-woof! Woof-woof! Woof-woof!
Jocasta **Michelangelo** **Giovanni** }	(*Astonished*) The secret of eternal life!
Michelangelo	We snatched the bowl from the dog and drank it down.

*   **Jocasta, Michelangelo** and **Giovanni** taste the potion in turn. It has the same electrifying effect as on the dog (**Amelia**).*

Michelangelo	Zing!
Jocasta	Zing!
Giovanni	Zing!
Amelia	(*Becoming human and taking the 'bowl' off Giovanni*) But we saved some…

> *Michelangelo grabs the 'bowl' and takes another quick swig. Amelia grabs it back and peers to see how much is left.*

Amelia	…a little – for Geoffrey Chaucer!
Alchemists	(*With over-the-top admiration*) The greatest poet in the land!
Jocasta	(*Confessing the truth*) We owed him a lot of money!

> *The Alchemists approach the comatose Geoffrey. Still miming the bowl, they feed the potion to Geoffrey while telling the story to the audience.*

Giovanni	When we arrived at his house he was just breathing his last breath.
Jocasta	We forced the potion between his lips.
Amelia	It was almost too late.
Jocasta	He was almost dead!
Giovanni	Now he is almost alive!

> *Jocasta and Michelangelo move downstage to talk to the audience. As they do so, Giovanni and Amelia stand Geoffrey up using the shroud to hide him from the audience.*

Jocasta	(*Switching to speak in American horror movie style*) Frozen in a strange and mystical comatose state between this world and the next.

Michelangelo	(*Switching back to showbiz style*) But not for long!

Jocasta   No, because tonight, before your very eyes, we are going to bring him completely back to life! Tonight the guest of honour is…

> *There is a loud fanfare (of voices or instruments) as **Giovanni** and **Amelia** pull away Geoffrey's shroud.*

Alchemists   Geoffrey Chaucer!

Michelangelo   (*To the audience*) Do we have a seat for Geoffrey? Who will have the honour of sitting next to one of England's finest half-dead poets?

Jocasta   (*To the audience*) For nearly six hundred years we have been trying to rouse him from his dreamless sleep!

> *Giovanni and Amelia take Geoffrey into the audience.*

Michelangelo   (*To the audience*) Today may be the day he wakes up next to you!

> *Giovanni and Amelia prop Geoffrey up in an empty seat.*

Amelia   (*To the audience member on Geoffrey's left*) He sneezes sometimes. I hope you won't mind wiping his nose.

Giovanni   (*To the audience member on Geoffrey's right*) Hold his hand. It might make him feel more lively.

> *Amelia and Giovanni start to go back to the stage.*

Amelia   If he moves – tell us right away!

Jocasta   (*Pointing from the stage*) He moved! He moved!

Amelia   It's the excitement!

*Amelia and Giovanni rush back to
Geoffrey and try some mimed 'electric pad'
heart stimulation on him.*

Giovanni   (*After a couple of jolts*) It's no use.

*Giovanni and Amelia run back to the
stage to join Michelangelo and Jocasta.*

Jocasta   (*To Geoffrey's neighbours in the audience*) Look after him will you. Feed him some crisps. We're going to try the treatment!

Michelangelo   (*In a horror style voice*) The treatment!

Jocasta   (*Keen and enthusiastic*) We're going to perform one of his very own Canterbury tales!

Michelangelo   (*More horror style*) In our own special way!

Amelia   (*Cheerfully*) That should wake him up!

The Pardoner's Tale

*The **Alchemists** perform an up-beat,
showbiz introduction for the Pardoner.*

Jocasta   Ladies and gentlemen – the Pardoner's Tale.

Giovanni   The pardon seller from Charing Cross with his yellow hair like rats' tails.

Amelia   The man with a voice like cream and honey.

Michelangelo   The famous holy relic seller straight from Italy.

Giovanni   Via Charing Cross!

Amelia   With letters of forgiveness signed by the Pope in Rome.

Jocasta   At a price!

Michelangelo   The man with the power to forgive your sins.

Jocasta	At a price!
Amelia	The one and only…
Alchemists	Priceless Pardoner!

*Facing the audience the **Alchemists** produce kazoos and play a grand and completely over-the-top fanfare. They do not see the **Pardoner** slip between the booth curtains and appear on the edge of the booth. He carries shoulder bags containing his relics and pardons. **Jocasta** suddenly becomes aware of the Pardoner's presence and stops playing the fanfare. The others stop too.*

Jocasta   (*On the kazoo*) Uh-oh!

*The **Alchemists** spin round and run to kneel by the booth. The **Pardoner** raises his arms, scans the whole audience, and chants in Latin.*

Pardoner   Radix malorum est cupiditas! (*He pauses for effect*) That's Latin you know. It means, 'the love of money is the root of evil'. It means greed, the endless desire for more and more wealth!

*The **Alchemists** become the Pardoner's assistants. They get up and set to work instantly to convince the audience.*

Amelia   More pounds to the dollar, more Porsches, more Peugeots!

Jocasta   More pockets full of plastic, more personal computers!

Michelangelo   More designer jeans with designer holes!

Giovanni	More designer trainers with designer soles!
Pardoner	(*Preaching to the whole audience*) And I know just how evil the love of money is dear brethren – it's my favourite sin! Yes, dear friends, the music that lifts my heart is the sound of the money I make by selling you pardon for your sins.

*The **Alchemists** fall to their knees.*

Alchemists	Amen!
Pardoner	So you go to heaven – while I go to hell. Not that I care where you go, you suckers, you sinners, you drunkards, you gluttons, you gamblers, you swearers and blasphemers, you lecherous swine! I can see the flames of hell licking around your ankles!
Alchemists	(*Raising their hands to heaven*) Hallelujah!
Pardoner	You are poor lost sheep.
Alchemists	(*Now on their hands and knees*) Baaaaaaaa!

*The **Alchemists** get up.*

Pardoner	But don't despair!

*The **Pardoner** takes off his shoulder bags, and passes one to the **Alchemists**, who start to unpack it eagerly while he continues to preach to the audience.*

Pardoner	If you've money to pay, your sins will be forgiven! (*He produces a scroll*) I've got pardons for sale signed by the Pope himself.

*Instantly, the **Alchemists** display other relics to the audience.*

Amelia	(*Displaying a box of matches*) A box of splinters from Noah's Ark!
Pardoner	(*Holding up an apple with two bites missing*) An apple from the garden of Eden!

Michelangelo	(*Producing a bottle of red-coloured water*) Water from the Red Sea!
Giovanni	(*Producing a bottle of black-coloured water*) Water from the Black Sea!
Jocasta	(*Producing a bottle of blue-coloured water*) Water from Galilee, guaranteed walked upon. Take some home and try it for yourself!

> ***Amelia*** *takes a mouldy-looking relic to the front row of the audience.*

Amelia	Here is St Christopher's toe bone – only ten pence a kiss!
Jocasta	(*Reacting as if she has heard a comment from someone in the audience*) What do you mean – it looks like a pig's foot?
Pardoner	(*Fiercely to the audience*) You'll go to hell for blasphemy!
Giovanni	(*Producing another larger bone*) Here is a shoulder bone from one of Jacob's sheep!
Michelangelo	Completely natural.
Jocasta	Additive free!
Pardoner	It'll cure the itch and the scritch, the pox and the scab, infertility, jealousy… (*He searches for something else to say about it*) …jealousy …infertility…
Giovanni	(*Struck with sudden inspiration*) It'll make damn good soup! A little pinch of salt, some pepper…
Pardoner	(*Interrupting*) And, if you're very poor, don't worry. I'll be happy to take your last penny so that I can eat and drink and have a girl in every town – while you starve for the good of your souls.

> *There is a snatch of music (e.g. bing, bong) as the* ***Alchemists*** *make an instant all-smiling tableau displaying the 'goods for sale'.*

Michelangelo	(*Through his smile*) They're not convinced!

Pardoner	(*To the audience*) I can see you're not convinced. Let me tell you a story.
	*The **Alchemists** scurry away to sit and watch from the sides of the stage. The **Pardoner** goes to the stage left pulpit and rings the story bell. **Tom**, **Dick** and **Harry** enter behind him. They appear to be drunk.*
Pardoner	Once upon a time in the middle of the Middle Ages, there lived four wild, riotous, drunken young hooligans.
	***Dick** takes out a large dagger, **Harry**, a middle-sized one, and **Tom**, a small one. They threaten the Pardoner with their weapons.*
Dick	Who do you think you're talkin' about, rabbit-face?
Harry	Give us a drink, smoothychops!
Tom	Give us some money or we'll cut off yer collywobbles!
Pardoner	(*Sternly, with authority*) And their names were…
	*The **Pardoner** uses a different percussion instrument for each of the young hooligans before they speak their name.*
Tom	(*Like a keen young fool*) Tom!
Dick	(*Like a thug*) Dick!
Harry	(*Laughing because he thinks he's funny*) Harry!
Pardoner	And Ambrosius!
	***Tom**, **Dick** and **Harry** realize that Ambrosius isn't there.*
Pardoner	Where was the leader of the gang? Where was (*The **Pardoner** makes a 'cool' sound with the percussion*) Ambrosius?

Harry goes to look for Ambrosius in the audience.

Dick   (*Calling from the stage*) Ambrosius!

Tom   (*Also calling from the stage*) Ambrosius!

Harry   (*Spotting him and pointing*) There he is!

*Harry picks someone to be Ambrosius from the audience. He brings them onto the stage and helps them to put on a jerkin, hat and knife belt. Meanwhile **Dick** and **Tom** describe the events of the previous night to the audience.*

Dick   Hey, Ambrosius, what a night last night eh?

Tom   (*To the audience*) He was drinkin' it outa the barrel! He was dancin' on the table!

Dick   Peein' out of the church steeple!

Tom   Chasin' the landlord's daughter!

Dick   Chasin' the landlord!

Tom   He was really drunk!

Dick   (*To Ambrosius*) Oh, yeah! D'you remember nuttin' that tax collector?

Tom   An' him sayin' he was goin' to tell the sheriff an' get you hung for it?

Dick   So you stuck his head in the pigswill – an' you said, 'Tell the sheriff I'll do the same for him…

Tom   …an' the king…

Dick   …an' all his army'!

*Tom, Dick and Harry surround
Ambrosius and give him lots of over-the-top
praise as they present him to the audience.*

Tom	Ambrosius! The tall, strong, good-looking, brainy, confident, leader of the gang!
Dick	Ambrosius! The well-dressed, trendy, smart, mean, cool, leader of the pack!
Harry	Ladies and gentlemen – Ambrosius!

*Everyone claps and cheers. The gang move to
sit at the table. One of the cast places a tray
with goblets and a pair of large dice on the
table.*

Harry	Take my seat, Ambrosius.
Dick	No, take mine.
Tom	You're the greatest, Ambrosius.

*Taking a bottle, the **Pardoner** crosses the
stage to swing out a pub sign hinged on the
booth – a skull and bones, mostly hidden
under a black, ragged, cloth hood.*

Pardoner	All day long they eat and drink – at a pub called Death's Arms.
Tom	What are you drinking, Ambrosius?
Harry	(*To the Pardoner*) Fill 'em up, landlord!

*The **Pardoner** pours the drinks. **Tom,
Dick** and **Harry** toast Ambrosius in turn,
throwing back full goblets of wine.*

Dick	Cheers!
Harry	Good health!
Tom	Down the hatch!

Dick	Bottoms up!
Harry	Mud in yer eye!
Dick	Rats in yer ears!
Tom	One for the road!
Pardoner	They eat and drink and start to gamble – at cards, at pitch and toss, at dice.

*The **Pardoner** passes the dice to Dick, and then returns to his pulpit.*

Dick	(*At first, nicely*) Little dice, please be nice (*Then aggressively*) or I'll knock spots off yer!

He kisses the dice, and throws them on the table. It's a good score.

Dick	I've won! I've won!
Harry	Hold yer horses! (*He passes the dice to Ambrosius*) Your throw, Ambrosius.

***Ambrosius** gets ready to throw. **Tom** and **Harry** chant his name.*

Tom } **Harry** }	Am-bro-si-us! Am-bro-si-us!

***Ambrosius** throws the dice. It's an even better score.*

Tom } **Harry** }	Yeeeees!
Dick	(*Glumly*) I've lost! I've lost!
Pardoner	They began to dance – wild, wicked and dirty dancing!

*There is music as **Tom**, **Dick**, **Ambrosius**, and **Harry** conga downstage and do the hokey cokey as a chorus line.*

Cast	You put yer left leg in, yer left leg out. You do the hokey cokey and you shake it all about!

*Then, **Tom**, **Dick**, and **Harry** lead or carry **Ambrosius** around the stage, singing to the tune of 'God Save the Queen'.*

Tom **Dick** **Harry**	God bless Ambrosius. He is the best of us! He's one of us! La la la la la…

*The dancing is too much for the gang on top of the eating and drinking. They reach the table and fall in a heap behind it. **Tom**, **Dick**, **Harry**, and **Ambrosius** groan, moan and make vomiting noises. Then they pass out.*

Pardoner	(*To the audience*) Aren't they awful? (*He pauses to allow for any reply from the audience*) And you're no different! (*Picking on a small section of the audience*) Where were you last night? Clubbing and pubbing and drinking strong ale? And afterwards you wake up in the morning and you cry, 'Fye! Alas! Oh stinking cod! What day is it? Where am I? Where have I been? What have I been doing – and who have I been doing it with?'.

There are groans, snorts and snores from the sleeping gang.

Pardoner	(*To the audience as he goes to get Ambrosius*) That night poor Ambrosius woke up and staggered to the lavatory. (*To Ambrosius*) Stagger Ambrosius! (*To the audience*) But alas, on the way, he died – of a massive heart attack! (*To Ambrosius*) Die Ambrosius!

Ambrosius, with encouragement from the cast and the audience, dies melodramatically.

Pardoner	(*Helping **Ambrosius** up from the floor and taking off his costume*) And so Ambrosius went off to the other world where a seat was waiting for him. A big clap for Ambrosius!

	*The **Pardoner** hangs up Ambrosius's costume. There is applause from the audience and the cast as **Ambrosius** goes back to his seat.*
Pardoner	(*Returning to the stage left pulpit*) When the other three hooligans woke up, it was very early in the morning.
	*The cast do birdsong impressions. **Tom**, **Dick** and **Harry** get up from behind the table.*
Pardoner	They were in a terrible state.
Dick	Red eyes! Shaking hands!
Tom	Dizzy brain! Dry mouth!
Harry	My tongue tastes like a courtier's cod piece!
	***Tom, Dick** and **Harry** groan and make other noises to suggest that they have awful hangovers. The **Pardoner** rings a loud funeral toll on a bell on his pulpit. **Tom**, **Dick** and **Harry** react instantly and try to cover their ears with their hands. Gradually, the bell stops. **Harry** removes his hands.*
Harry	Sounds like some poor serf has kicked the bucket.
Tom } Dick }	(*With their hands still over their ears*) Eh?
Harry	(*Shouting*) Dead!!!!
	***Tom** and **Dick** take their hands off their ears, and look around at everybody.*
Tom } Dick }	Who?
Pardoner	Ambrosius!

| Tom Dick Harry | (*Realizing that Ambrosius is missing*) Ambrosius! |

Dick   (*Looking under the table*) I wondered where he'd gone to!

> **Tom**, **Dick** and **Harry** *surround the*
> **Pardoner** *in his pulpit.*

Tom   Who killed him? Was it you?

Dick   We'll cut your throat if you don't confess!

Harry   We'll cut your throat if you do confess!

> *The* **Pardoner** *leaves the stage left pulpit*
> *and walks to the table. As he does he speaks*
> *forcefully to Tom, Dick and Harry.*

Pardoner   It wasn't me! Your poor old friend was sitting on the bench,
                    dead drunk – but still alive – when Death crept up behind
                    him. (*He climbs onto the bench*) He was killed… (*He throws the*
                    hood off the pub sign to reveal the skull) …by Death!

> **Tom**, **Dick** and **Harry** *are terrified. With*
> *the* **Pardoner**, *they begin a trance-like*
> *chant, possibly accompanied by a drum and*
> *drone.*

| Tom Dick Harry | Death |

Pardoner   His bony arms!

| Tom Dick Harry | Death! |

Pardoner   His hollow eyes!

| Tom Dick Harry | Death! |

Pardoner	His gaping jaw!
Tom **Dick** **Harry**	Death!
Pardoner	His rancid breath!
Tom **Dick** **Harry**	Death!
Pardoner	The plague is in his touch!
Tom **Dick** **Harry**	(*Coming out of their trance*) What's that to us?
Pardoner	Men, women, children, whole villages die – when Death passes by.
Tom **Dick** **Harry**	What's that to us?
Pardoner	(*Meaningfully*) Ambrosius!

*The **Pardoner** walks back to his pulpit.*

Tom	(*In shock, looking around*) Death – everywhere!
Pardoner	That's what my mother says.
Dick	A pox on your mother!
Harry	If she hasn't got the pox already!
Dick	(*Climbing onto the table*) I'm not frightened by this Death character! Where is he? I'll kill him!
Tom	(*With bravado, climbing onto a bench next to Dick*) Me too! By Saint Gregory's elbow! Revenge for Ambrosius! Death to Death!

Harry	(*Joining Dick and Tom*) By God's teeth! This Death is as good as dead!
Dick	We swear an oath.
Tom	We swear a solemn oath.
	They spit on their hands and clasp them all together.
Tom **Dick** **Harry** }	Death to Death!
	*Tom, Dick and Harry climb down and race off into the audience. They approach people and demand that they tell them where Death is. As they leave the stage, an **old man** enters stage left. He is wrapped in a blanket, and carries a walking stick. Slowly, he moves across the stage, banging the ground with his stick. **Tom, Dick** and **Harry** are fully occupied with the audience and do not see the old man straight away.*
Tom	(*To the audience*) Anyone here seen Death?
Harry	(*Pointing to an audience member*) He looks like Death over there!
Dick	(*Questioning an audience member*) Are you Death, mister?
	*Before anyone can reply to Dick's question, the **Pardoner** beats a drum. **Dick** turns to see the old man.*
Dick	Here – Tom, Harry – look at that old geezer up there!
Tom	I can smell him from here!
Harry	(*Shouting from the audience*) Oi! Come here! I'm talking to you, you deaf old git!
	*The **old man** pauses in his tracks.*

Old Man	(*Peering at the hooligans in the audience*) God save and keep you, gentlemen!
Dick	Go to hell, you old scarecrow! You should be in your grave, an old bloke like you!
Tom	What are you doing still wandering about like some walking blanket?
Old Man	Because I can't find any young lad like you who'd like to exchange his youth for my age. Even Death won't take my life! (*Banging the ground with his stick*) Mother! Dearest Mother! Let me in! See how I'm wasting, flesh and blood and skin! (*To the gang*) But Mother Earth won't take me in her arms!
Harry	I wouldn't take you in my arms neither, you smelly old git!
	Harry laughs like a hyena; he thinks he's said something really funny.
Old Man	You shouldn't speak to me like that! How would you like to be treated when you are my age?
Tom	I'd rather die than end up like you!
Old Man	Then God be with you. I'm going on my way!
	*The **old man** continues on his way from stage left to stage right, but **Tom**, **Dick** and **Harry** race from the audience onto the stage and waylay him.*
Dick	Not so fast by St John's eyeball.
	***Dick** kicks away the old man's stick so that he falls to the ground. Then, the three hooligans surround the old man and continue to question him as he struggles onto the bench by the table.*
Dick	What do you know of this Mister Death?
Tom	You must be one of his spies. Where is he?

Harry	You're a friend of Death! You want to kill all us young people because you're old and jealous!
	Dick grabs the old man's stick and threatens him with it.
Dick	By God and the Pope's breakfast, tell us where Death is or I'll...
	*The **old man** has had enough. He stops Dick in mid-threat.*
Old Man	(*Interrupting*) You want to find Death? Then follow this winding road until you come to a tall oak tree. I saw Death there just an hour ago. Go! And God mend your ways!
	*The **old man** points the opposite way to the path he's been travelling. **Dick** drops the stick. **Tom**, **Dick** and **Harry** pull out their daggers and race round the back of the booth. The **old man** opens the booth curtains, revealing a canvas with a large oak tree painted on it. At the foot of the tree, are six sacks, marked 'gold'. The **old man** picks up his stick and exits. We can hear **Tom**, **Dick** and **Harry** whooping and calling from behind the booth. The **Pardoner** continues the narration from the stage left pulpit.*
Pardoner	Tom, Dick and Harry ran to the tree with daggers drawn.
	***Tom**, **Dick** and **Harry** race on from stage right, brandishing their daggers.*
Tom	There it is!
	***Tom**, **Dick** and **Harry** climb onto the booth.*
Pardoner	But when they arrived at the oak, instead of finding Death sitting in its shade, they found...
Dick	(*Picking up one of the sacks*) Lots of old bags!

They put their daggers away. **Tom** *and* **Harry** *start to open one of the bags.*

Harry   What's in them?

Tom   What's inside them?

Dick   Let me guess! (*He grabs a bag and feels it with his eyes shut*) Flour. No. Frogs! Sausages! I know – dead bodies all chopped up in pieces!

Harry brings out some coins.

Harry   Gold.

Tom
Dick   (*Sitting down to examine the coins*) Gold!
Harry

Pardoner   So much gold that they had to sit and gaze at it for a while.

Tom   (*Holding a coin to let the sun glint on it*) Wow!

Harry   (*Rubbing a coin on his face*) Wow!

Dick   (*Sticking a coin in each eye*) Oh wow!

Harry   Listen! I know I'm a bit of a joker, but the sight of this gold makes me feel... very serious. (*He gets carried away*) There's enough here to let us live in luxury for ever and ever... (*He pulls out his dagger*) ...and it's all mine!

Dick pulls out his dagger and points it at Harry.

Dick   All ours!

Tom   (*Drawing his dagger then deciding to pick on the audience instead*) And... and nobody else's!

Harry   (*Collecting all their daggers together*) We'll draw daggers! The one with the shortest dagger has to go and buy us food and wine while the other two guard the gold till night falls!

*Harry holds the daggers out together to Tom. **Dick** and **Harry** quickly make sure Tom gets the short dagger.*

Tom   Hey – I've drawn the short dagger, I have!

*They put their daggers away. **Harry** gives Tom some gold pieces.*

Harry   Here you are! And don't forget the chicken pies!

*As **Tom** gets down from the booth, and starts to leave, stage right, **Dick** shouts at him.*

Dick   And don't forget the wine!

Harry   I want salt and vinegar and lots of sauce on my pies!

Dick   And don't forget the wine!

Harry   And make sure the pies are hot!

Dick   (*Just as **Tom** goes off*) And Tom!

Tom   (*Returning, exasperated*) What?

Dick   Don't forget the pies!

*Tom leaves. **Dick** and **Harry** laugh at their own pathetic joke. **Dick** suddenly lies back and starts snoring.*

Pardoner   As soon as Tom was out of sight, Harry had some thoughts.

*As **Dick** sleeps, **Harry** counts the bags of gold. Thinking comes hard for Harry.*

Harry   One two! One two! One two! – Hmmm! One two three. One two three. Heh heh! Heh heh! Heh heh! (*He prods Dick*) Dick!

Dick starts awake, and draws his dagger.

Dick   What?

Harry	(*Showing Dick by moving the bags*) A pile of gold divided between two is a lot more each than a pile of gold divided between three!
Dick	(*Beginning to understand*) Oh yeah.

He puts his dagger away.

Harry	And two is stronger than one.
Dick	(*Excited*) Yeah!
Harry	So when Tom gets back from town with the wine and pies and sits down for a rest…
Dick	(*Wildly excited*) We'll grab him!
Harry	Like we're joking!
Dick	Ha, ha!
Harry	Yeah – and I'll stick my dagger in his back!
Dick	(*Completely carried away*) And I'll do the same – and then we'll cut his body into little pieces and put it in the sacks and take all the gold and go out gambling and drinking – and everything!
Harry	(*Unsettled a little by Dick*) Yeah.
Dick	Great!

*Exhausted with the mental effort, **Dick** and **Harry** stretch out to sleep. **Tom** enters, stage left.*

Pardoner	Meanwhile, young Tom was walking to town. On the way he had a little thought.

*There is a 'ding' from the percussion. **Tom** freezes as the idea hits him.*

Tom	If only I could have all that gold for myself – what a happy lad I would be!

Pardoner	And then a little devil had a little word in his little ear. And the word was…
Tom	(*To the audience with wicked relish*) Poison!

> The **Pardoner** *produces a bottle of poison from his pulpit and becomes the poison seller.* **Tom** *approaches him.*

Pardoner	A very strong and deadly poison! (**Tom** *reaches eagerly for the bottle*) But remember, this is for sporting and hunting purposes only.
Tom	It's not for me! It's for …some friends.

> The **Pardoner** *gives Tom the poison and crosses to the stage right pulpit ahead of Tom.*

Pardoner	(*To the audience*) Next, Tom went to the wine sellers (*He picks up three bottles from the pulpit*) and bought three bottles of wine.

> The **Pardoner** *gives Tom the bottles.* **Tom** *looks curiously at him as he takes the bottles.*

Tom	Thanks.

> **Tom** *looks across to where he bought the poison and then back to the Pardoner. He is confused.*

Tom	(*To the Pardoner*) Haven't I seen you somewhere before?

> **Tom** *looks back to the stage left pulpit, and then back to the Pardoner.*

Pardoner	(*Explaining*) My brother!

> **Tom** *accepts this. He mimes to the Pardoner's narration with the bottles and poison.*

Pardoner	Tom shared the deadly poison between two of the bottles and then made his way back to the old oak tree, making sure all the time that he kept the two poisoned bottles in one hand and the unpoisoned bottle in the other.
Tom	(*Chuckling gleefully to the audience*) Heh, heh, heh!

> *Dick and Harry are still asleep. Tom calls to them from downstage of the booth.*

Tom	(*Putting on a ridiculously innocent expression*) Dick! Harry! I'm back!

> *Startled awake, Dick and Harry sit up, and then come down to join Tom.*

Harry	Eh?
Dick	What?
Harry	Where's the chicken pies?
Tom	Oh no! I forgot! (*He passes them the bottles*) Drink the wine and I'll go back for them!

> *Dick and Harry put their wine down and Harry puts his arm round Tom.*

Harry	(*Drawing his dagger*) Don't worry about the pies, Tommy boy! You have a nice rest!
Dick	(*Drawing his dagger*) Have a nice long rest!

> *Together, they stab Tom in the back. Tom is rigid with shock. As they pull their daggers out, he falls to the floor.*

Tom	Aaaaaaaaaaaaaaaaargh!

> *In his death throes, Tom beckons Harry closer.*

Tom	(*In a hoarse whisper*) Harry!

| Harry | Yeah? |

| Tom | I'm sorry about the pies! |

*With those words, **Tom** dies. **Dick** and **Harry** laugh.*

| Harry | Nice one, Dick! |

| Dick | Yeah! |

| Harry | Let's have a drink to celebrate our partnership, before we bury him. |

| Dick | Before we chop… |

| Harry | (*Interrupting, not wanting to hear Dick's grisly plan*) Yeah, yeah! |

***Dick** and **Harry** pick up their bottles to take a swig. They raise them to the audience.*

| Dick
Harry } | Cheers! |

***Dick** and **Harry** raise their daggers behind each other's backs ready to stab each other – but, as they swig the wine, they freeze, glassy-eyed! The **Pardoner** crosses the stage and takes the bottles out of their unmoving hands. He speaks as he moves.*

| Pardoner | And of course the poison was just as strong as the apothecary had said it was, strong enough to kill two rats, two stoats, two weasels – or even two large polecats! |

***Dick** and **Harry** drop and die in three quick convulsions.*

| Dick
Harry } | Urgh! Aaagh! Ugh! |

*Three bodies now lie flat out on the floor. The **Pardoner** puts down the bottles and picks up a bag of gold. He climbs onto the table and addresses the audience.*

Pardoner	Ladies and gentlemen, as you meditate on the corpses of these three, lively, young people, lying dead here around the old oak tree with the pile of gold in the middle, think on this: if you go looking for Death – don't be surprised if you find him!

> *There is music as* **Tom**, **Dick** *and* **Harry** *leap to their feet and take a bow. They invite Ambrosius to take a bow from his seat.*

Tom
Dick } Ambrosius!
Harry

Interlude

> **Tom**, **Dick** *and* **Harry** *exit. The* **Pardoner** *closes the booth curtains but then turns suddenly on the audience.*

Pardoner Think also on your sins, your greed, your gluttony, your lechery! (*He builds to a crescendo*) Are you too seeking Death like Tom, Dick and Harry? Or are you seeking life? Are you coming back to the light? Are you going to rise again?

> *Giovanni suddenly leaps up from where he is sitting at the side of the stage and points at Geoffrey in the audience.*

Giovanni Geoffrey! I saw him breath!

> *The other three* **Alchemists** *stand up to look.*

Michelangelo He's rising again!

Amelia He's coming back to the light!

Giovanni (*To an audience member near Geoffrey*) Feel his pulse!

Jocasta (*To the same member of the audience*) Feel his heart! (*Pause*) No – higher up! His heart!

Michelangelo (*To Geoffrey's neighbours*) Keep your eye on him! We'll do another tale!

Pardoner	(*In an ominous voice*) Once upon a…
Michelangelo	(*Quickly interrupting*) Something less morbid!

*The **Pardoner** sniffs haughtily.*

Pardoner	Huh!

He exits through the booth.

Amelia	Something with danger, but no death!

*As they speak, the **Alchemists** move the table lengthwise, stage right, parallel to the front of the booth to provide a thrust. The two benches are placed end-on to improvise a narrow 'catwalk' from the downstage centre of the booth.*

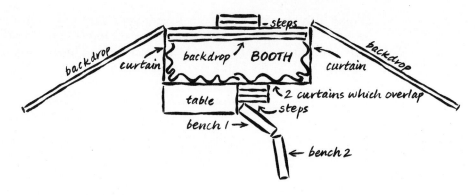

Giovanni	Something colourful and fabulous for all the family.
Jocasta	A story about animals and children.

There are various animal noises from the booth.

Jocasta	Well – animals, at least!

The Nun's Priest's Tale

Michelangelo   Ladies and gentlemen – the Nun's Priest's Tale!

*The **Nun's Priest** enters.
The **Alchemists** welcome him.
He blesses them, and they return
to their seats at the side of the stage.
As he walks to the stage right
pulpit, the **Nun's Priest** blesses
the audience. There is an immediate
contrast between his gentle humour
and the Pardoner's hell-raising style.*

Nun's Priest   (*To the audience*) Genial Brother John, that's what they call me
– the Nun's Priest. I live quietly in a convent full of holy nuns.
I say their mass each day and listen to their secret
confessions.(*He smiles and nods*) It's an interesting life – and
I've plenty of time spare to read, and think, and watch the
chickens in the yard.

*He forgets the audience for a moment and
starts to feed some imaginary hens.*

Nun's Priest   Here, chickchickchick, here, chickchickchick!

*He becomes aware of the audience again and
senses that they may have been laughing at
him.*

Nun's Priest   (*Defensively*) There are many lessons to be learned from God's
innocent animals… (*firmly and confidently*) … and this is one
of them!

*The **Nun's Priest** rings the story bell on the
pulpit, allowing the sound to die away before
he begins his tale.*

Nun's Priest   Once there was a noble cock called Chaunticleer who belonged to a poor widowed countrywoman and her two daughters.

> *Chaunticleer puts his head between the front curtains of the booth and squawks. He wears a 'cockerel' mask.*

Nun's Priest   Chaunticleer, a proud and handsome cock!

> *Chaunticleer comes out from between the curtains and starts to strut back and forth along the table in front of the booth.*

Nun's Priest   Chaunticleer had a loud and beautiful voice and was always crowing loudly in the chicken yard… (*Chaunticleer crows and struts down the 'cat-walk'*) … from early in the morning… (*Chaunticleer crows again as he struts to the end of the 'cat-walk'*) …till late at night.

> *Chaunticleer gives a really loud cock-a-doodle-do from the end of the 'cat-walk'. Immediately, there are shouts from behind the booth curtain.*

Voice 1   Shut the racket!

Voice 2   Go to sleep!

> *Chaunticleer's pride is hurt. He reacts by squawking and preening himself.*

Nun's Priest   Chaunticleer had many hens (*Chaunticleer perks up*) but his favourite was called Pertelote.

> *The Nun's Priest pauses expectantly, but there is no sign of Pertelote. He tries again.*

Nun's Priest   A proud and beautiful hen of good birth.

> *Pertelote appears through the booth curtains. She wears a 'hen' mask. She preens and clucks and settles on the table, giving the eye to Chaunticleer who struts back to join her.*

He cradles her head in his 'wing' and sings a gentle lullaby to his favourite hen. He sings unaccompanied, in the style of a simple folk song.

Chaunticleer   Westron wind, when wilt thou blow?
The small rain down can rain.
Christ, if my love were in my arms,
and I in my bed again.

*As **Chaunticleer** finishes the song, he and **Pertelote** snuggle together, as if on a perch, and fall asleep. The **Nun's Priest** continues his narration. He uses percussion instruments to create nightmarish sound effects as he describes Chaunticleer's dream.*

Nun's Priest   However, that night, Chaunticleer's sleep was disturbed by a dreadful dream, a terrible nightmare of a beast, something like a dog, but not a dog, with yellow-red fur, black tips to its tail and ears, and two fierce burning eyes!

*The **Nun's Priest** ends with a crash on a cymbal. This wakes **Chaunticleer**, who makes terrible cockerel-like calls of alarm, which in turn wakes **Pertelote**.*

Nun's Priest   On awakening, he tried to tell Pertelote of the terrible thing he'd dreamed.

*Using mime and clucking noises, **Chaunticleer** tries to show Pertelote the terrible beast from his nightmare. **Pertelote** doesn't understand this charade at all and **Chaunticleer** becomes more and more frustrated. Finally, he is forced to speak.*

Chaunticleer   Fox – you idiot! Fox!

Nun's Priest   Pertelote wasn't at all impressed.

Pertelote

(*Taking charge*) Pull yourself together, you silly bird! There is no truth whatsoever in dreams! Nightmares are caused by a sickness of the stomach. (*She slaps Chaunticleer in the stomach. He splutters and gurgles*) What you need is a purge! I shall mix you a medicine of ground worms and laxatives!

> *Pertelote begins to mime mixing the medicine. Chaunticleer takes a quick sniff of the mixture and rushes immediately down to the stage right pulpit to squawk complaint and make faces of disgust to the Nun's Priest. The Nun's Priest comes up with a solution.*

Nun's Priest

(*Calming Chaunticleer*) All right! All right! (*He returns to his story*) Just the THOUGHT of swallowing the laxatives made Chaunticleer feel a lot better very quickly!

> *Chaunticleer gets the idea and starts strutting around confidently.*

Nun's Priest

He was soon strutting round the yard like his usual self.

> *Chaunticleer crows loudly and behaves in a macho cockerel way. Pertelote beckons him seductively. She goes behind the booth curtains. Chaunticleer follows her.*

Nun's Priest

That night, however, while Chaunticleer and Pertelote were busy fertilizing some free range eggs (*Crows and clucks from behind the curtains*) Chaunticleer's dreadful dream came vibrantly to life.

> *There is the noise of cans and rattling of dustbin lids from the back of the auditorium. Sir Russell Fox enters from the back of the audience. He wears a 'fox' mask. He calls out.*

Sir Russell Fox

(*Barking*) I am no dream!

> *There is a musical percussion accompaniment as Sir Russell Fox races down to the stage. He freezes for a moment before introducing himself to the audience. He's a real smoothie.*

| **Sir Russell Fox** | I am Sir Russell Fox. |

Sir Russell Fox slinks quickly across the stage to hide in the stage left pulpit.

| **Nun's Priest** | The next day Chaunticleer awoke early. |

Chaunticleer crows as he appears from between the booth curtains.

| **Nun's Priest** | He went off to the cabbage patch to peck... |

Chaunticleer looks disdainfully at the Nun's Priest.

| **Nun's Priest** | ... and peck... |

Chaunticleer approaches the Nun's Priest with a meaningful look in his eye.

| **Nun's Priest** | ... and peck... |

Chaunticleer stares at the Nun's Priest until he realizes what the cock is driving at.

| **Nun's Priest** | ...oh, and to sing. |

Chaunticleer, well pleased now, struts operatically downstage centre. He clears his throat and sings, for the audience, in the style of a great opera singer.

Chaunticleer

I am a noble co-o-ock.
I crow at the break of da-a-ay.
I rise up every morning
My matins for to say.

I am a noble co-o-ock.
The finest rooster ye-e-et!
My comb is of red coral
And my tail is black as je-e-e-e-et!

Chaunticleer   I am a noble co-o-ock.
My eyes do glow like a-a-a-amber.
And every night I perch u-up high
In my lady's chamb…er.

> *Chaunticleer extends the last syllable of 'chamber', singing up and down the scale. While **Chaunticleer** is doing this, **Sir Russell Fox** creeps up on him. **Chaunticleer** is really showing off in operatic style. Suddenly, mid-note, he sees Sir Russell Fox and ends with a terrible gurgle.*

Chaunticleer   Fox! Glurk! Fox!

> *'Silent movie' music accompanies **Chaunticleer** as he makes an effort to escape from Sir Russell Fox. They run round and round the stage and/or auditorium, leaping over the 'cat-walk', in the style of a comic chase routine. **Sir Russell Fox** never gets close enough to grab Chaunticleer and is soon out of breath. Finally, they both stop to rest, and collapse quite close to each other.*

Nun's Priest   It was Sir Russell Fox, a sly creature, who spoke these words…

> *Chaunticleer jumps up, ready to race off again.*

Sir Russell Fox   (*In an oily voice*) Don't run away. I'm an opera fan! I've come to listen to your beautiful voice.

Chaunticleer   (*Surprised and flattered*) Oh!

Sir Russell Fox   I knew your dear father well, you know. They used to say he was the best singing cock in the whole world – but I think your voice might be even better than his.

> *Chaunticleer squirms with pleasure.*

Sir Russell Fox	Sing for me, so that I can judge for myself. Sing! Sing!
	Chauncicleer moves downstage. He speaks to Sir Russell Fox but faces the audience.
Chaunticleer	Just listen to this.
Nun's Priest	Chaunticleer stood on his toes and stretched his neck.
Sir Russell Fox	(*Drooling*) Yes! Stretch it for me. Stretch it!
Nun's Priest	With open mouth and rattling tonsils, he sang aloud to the world with pride!
	Chaunticleer sings a musical scale in the style of an over-the-top, Italian opera.
Chaunticleer	Do ray me fa so la ti do.
Sir Russell Fox	Again! Again! What a tasty voice!
	Chaunticleer sings again, holding the last note and possibly continuing with more improvised 'opera'.
Chaunticleer	Do ray me fa so la ti dooooooo.
Nun's Priest	(*Dramatically*) Just then, Sir Russell Fox grabbed Chaunticleer by the throat…
	Sir Russell Fox grabs Chaunticleer by the throat.
Chaunticleer	Glurk!
Nun's Priest	…and ran off with him to the wood!
	Sir Russell Fox throws Chaunticleer over his shoulder (a fireman's lift) and heads off around the back of the booth.
Nun's Priest	Pertelote and all the hens made loud uproar.

| | *Pertelote, squawking urgently, appears through the booth curtains. She opens the curtains to reveal the oak tree backdrop (from the Pardoner's Tale).* |

Nun's Priest   (*To the audience*) All the hens! Come on, let's hear you!

Pertelote comes down from the booth to join the Nun's Priest as everybody – cast and audience – starts to make clucking noises.

Nun's Priest   (*To the audience*) That's the idea! (*He continues the story*) The widowed countrywoman and her two daughters and all the villagers heard the noise and gave chase crying, 'Help! Help! The fox has stolen our cock!' All together (*He gestures to the audience to join in*).

All   'Help! Help! The fox has stolen our cock!'

There is a hunting fanfare.

Nun's Priest   A fox! A fox! Halloo! A fox!

Sir Russell Fox enters from behind the booth with Chaunticleer.

Nun's Priest   However, before they could catch up, the fox reached the safety of the wood.

Still carrying Chaunticleer, Sir Russell Fox stands in front of the booth. He gives a snarl of triumph. He then turns to 'enter the wood' and freezes for a moment.

Nun's Priest   Chaunticleer managed to speak.

Chaunticleer   (*Over Sir Russell Fox's shoulder*) Cock-a-doodle-do! You're safe now. They haven't caught you. And, even though I am to be your dinner, I must admit you are a clever fox.

Sir Russell Fox (*Back over his shoulder*) Clever fox! Clever!

Chaunticleer	Yes! And if I were you, I would turn and wave at the villagers and shout, 'Go away, you stupid yokels! I've got the cock now! And I'm going to eat him up'!

*Sir Russell Fox puts **Chaunticleer** down, turns, and calls to the audience. While he is doing this, **Chaunticleer** flaps off to find a safe perch on the table.*

Sir Russell Fox	Go away, you stupid yokels! (*Making a rude gesture*) I've got the cock now. And I'm going to eat him up!

*Sir Russell Fox turns back, finds **Chaunticleer** gone and is very angry. He looks fiercely about amongst the audience. **Chaunticleer** clucks and crows. Sir Russell Fox turns in the direction of the noise.*

Chaunticleer	Eat me up! Eat me up! No chance, you stupid fox! I am Chaunticleer, the greatest singing cock, the cleverest singing cock!

*Sir Russell Fox roars and barks with rage, but then pulls himself together and becomes oily and crafty. During Sir Russell Fox's speech, **Chaunticleer** continues to move closer and closer to Sir Russell Fox, allowing him to think that he has tricked the cock again.*

Sir Russell Fox	No! Wait! No! Alas! Dear Chaunticleer, I didn't mean to eat you. Just a joke, a little game. I just wanted to take you for a ride to the woods. Won't you come down and sing me another song? (*Pleading*) Come down. Sing for me.

*Just as **Chaunticleer** is within reach of Sir Russell Fox, he slashes at the cock with a paw, and **Chaunticleer** jumps back to safety, crowing triumphantly once again.*

Chaunticleer	No fear! I'll see us both damned first! (*Sir Russell Fox snarls with rage*) You won't trick me twice with your flattery!

Sir Russell Fox   (*To the audience, as he exits*) Shucks! I'd better go and raid some dustbins!

> *Sir Russell Fox exits through the audience. The sound of banging dustbin lids and tins is heard again as he leaves the auditorium. He swiftly and secretly races round backstage. Chaunticleer comes down onto the stage. Pertelote rushes to embrace him.*

Pertelote   Oh Chaunticleer, your dream came true. I'm glad it didn't run away with you!

> *Sir Russell Fox begins to creep up on Chaunticleer from backstage. The Nun's Priest leaves his pulpit and joins Pertelote and Chaunticleer. He addresses the audience as he does so.*

Nun's Priest   And that's the end of my tale, but remember to be on your guard against flatterers…

> *The Nun's Priest turns round and catches Sir Russell Fox as he is about to leap. Sir Russell Fox shrugs and stands aside, rather embarrassed. Chaunticleer opens his mouth to speak but the Nun's Priest continues, glaring at him.*

Nun's Priest   …and all those who open their mouths when they should keep them shut!

> *Chaunticleer shuts his mouth. The Nun's Priest finishes his tale, with the three beasts around him. The actors playing the hen, the cock and the fox unmask as they are named.*

Nun's Priest   (*To the audience*) And if you think my story is absurd, a silly fable of a beast or bird. A nonsense of a fox, a cock, a hen, then good luck to you, ladies and gentlemen!

> *All the actors bow. The cast and the audience applaud.*

Interlude

*The **Alchemists** walk on stage to congratulate the actors, shaking their hands and patting them on their backs. **Michelangelo** glances at Geoffrey.*

Michelangelo   He moved!

Everyone focuses on Geoffrey.

Giovanni   He twitched!

Jocasta   He picked his nose!

Amelia   He smiled at the animals!

Michelangelo   (*To everyone, excitedly*) It's working. Another tale, quick!

Giovanni   Nearly the interval!

Michelangelo   We'll see how far we get. Another pilgrim!

Jocasta   Someone full of life…

Amelia   Someone bursting with energy and vibrant sensuality!

*All the **Alchemists** have the same pilgrim in mind. They become very enthusiastic.*

Michelangelo   You mean (*Amelia nods*) right!

Jocasta   Right!

Giovanni   Let's go!

*The stage empties except for the **Alchemists** who start moving the set around. They turn the table end on so that it makes a longer, centre-booth thrust with the steps at the downstage end and the benches either side, slanted towards the audience. As they move things around, they introduce the next pilgrim to the audience.*

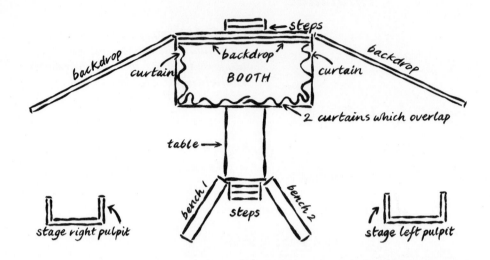

The Wife of Bath's Tale (Part One)

Michelangelo	Ladies and gentlemen, today's mystery guest is a woman of…
Alchemists	…experience!
Amelia	She's been on every package pilgrimage there is!
Jocasta	Jerusalem!
Giovanni	Rome!
Jocasta	Spain!
Michelangelo	Boulogne!
Amelia	She was born in Taurus under Mars and Venus.
Giovanni	Mars for energy…
Amelia	…and Venus for sensuality!
Jocasta	She's got a special mole of Venus in a very private place.
Wife of Bath	(*Speaking from behind the booth curtains*) I have an' all!

Michelangelo	Ladies and gentlemen.
Alchemists	(*As if introducing a pop star*) The Wife of Bath!

*The **Alchemists** move to the front of the stage and go into a big choreographed rock and roll introduction – Elvis style.*

Alchemists

Here comes the Wife of Bath.
She shook the Middle Ages
with her bawdy laugh.
The husbands that she married
dropped and died in disgrace.
None of them could sta-and the pace!
She was a liberated lady,
that Middle Ages baby.
Let's hear it for the Wife of Bath!

*The **Wife of Bath** enters from behind the booth curtains. She moves along the thrust-table, singing an even more punchy version of her introduction.*

Wife of Bath

Here I come, the Wife of Bath.
I shook the Middle Ages
with my bawdy laugh.
The husbands that I married
dropped and died in disgrace.
None of them could sta-and the pace!
Yes, I'm a liberated lady,
this Middle Ages baby.
Let's hear it for the Wife of Bath!

*By the end of her introduction, the **Wife of Bath** has joined the Alchemists at the front of the stage. They go into a more bluesy routine, with the **Wife of Bath** as the star turn and the **Alchemists** as her back-up group of 'boy dancers' who dance the roles and sing the chorus.*

Wife of Bath	Yes, I've got a mole of Venus.
	It's well hidden away.
	And one of you young men might catch
	A sight of it one day.
	I've got a gap between my teeth
	And that's a sign as well.
	It means I like, well, what I like,
	Lord save my soul from hell!
	I wear big hats. I like big men
	With energy to spare.
	How come they have such little brains
	Under all that hair?
Wife of Bath **Alchemists**	Yes, if you're very lucky
	And you're pretty and you're plucky
	You might make it with the Wife of Bath!
Wife of Bath	My first three husbands, they were rich,
	Rich and old and grey.
	I took their cash and wore them out
	And buried them next day!
	I'm really not ashamed of that.
	They had, I swear by God,
	A right good time before I put them
	Underneath the sod!
Wife of Bath **Alchemists**	Yes, if you're very lucky
	And you're pretty and you're plucky
	You might make it with the Wife of Bath!
Wife of Bath	My husband number four, I found
	A-sneakin' out of bed.
	He tried to make me jealous,
	Now that number four is dead.
	And on the day they buried him,
	My sinful soul God shrive,
	I licked my lips at the sexy legs
	Of husband number five.
Wife of Bath **Alchemists**	Yes, if you're very lucky
	And you're pretty and you're plucky
	You might make it with the Wife of Bath!

Wife of Bath	Now Jankin's my fifth husband. He isn't rich or old. He's got the balls; he's got the brains; He does just what he's told! But, if one day I find that boy Up to any tricks, Then step in line, 'cos now's the time For husband number six!
Wife of Bath **Alchemists**	Yes, if you're very lucky And you're pretty and you're plucky You might make it, you might make it, you might make it – – you might make it with the Wife of Bath!

> *The **Alchemists** and the cast lead the*
> *audience in noisy applause, whistles and*
> *cheers. The **Wife of Bath** responds to this*
> *and then turns on the men in the audience.*
> *She is provocative, but good humoured.*

Wife of Bath	You men are all hypocrites! You think I'm a wicked woman but King Solomon had lots of wives and so did Abraham and Jacob, so why shouldn't I have a few husbands? At least I have them one at a time! (*She pauses*) Virginity is a fine thing, as I'm sure you all agree, but God didn't make us male and female just so we could tell each other apart! (*There is another pause*) My little lambkins, I am a woman of experience and the most important thing I've learned is this – the world would be a better place, for all of us, if women had more power, if women had the mastery over men! (*She looks around the men in the audience*) Anybody want to argue? Good! Let me tell you a tale!

> *The **Alchemists** return to their seats at the*
> *side of the stage. The **Wife of Bath** crosses*
> *to the stage left pulpit and rings the story bell.*
> ***Sir Codsbrain** strides impatiently on stage.*
> *He is followed by his **squire**, who carries*
> *Sir Codsbrain's sword and is trying*
> *to finish dressing him.*

Wife of Bath	Once upon a time, the land of England was full of magic. And in those magic days of King Arthur and Queen Guinevere, there lived in England a manly, macho knight called Sir Codsbrain.

Sir Codsbrain (*To the female members of the audience*) Hello ladies! (*To the squire*) Stop dithering about, you half-wit.

> *Sir Codsbrain* takes his sword from the *squire* and kicks him ungraciously off stage.

Sir Codsbrain Go and polish the horses or something!

> *The* **squire** *exits.* **Sir Codsbrain** *starts showing off for the audience, performing martial exercises with his sword.*

Sir Codsbrain Huzzah! Huzzah! Huzzah! (*To a girl in the audience*) Impressive, eh?

Wife of Bath (*Breaking in quickly*) One day, Codsbrain was flying his hunting hawk down by the river…

Sir Codsbrain (*Miming releasing his hawk from his wrist*) Look! Bunny rabbits! Kill, Beelzebub, kill!

> **Amanda,** *the maiden, enters. She carries a wicker basket on her arm. She starts to mime picking raspberries off bushes.*

Wife of Bath …when he saw Amanda, a beautiful maiden, out on her own, picking raspberries.

> **Sir Codsbrain** *whistles and makes other stereotyped, sexist gestures towards Amanda. She ignores him.* **Sir Codsbrain** *approaches her, ready with his number one chat-up line.*

Sir Codsbrain I say! What's a lovely girl like you doing out all on her own?

Amanda Trying to keep away from dim-witted knights who ask stupid questions.

Sir Codsbrain Ha, ha, ha! I like a girl with a sense of humour! How would you like me to rescue you from a dragon?

Amanda What dragon, dung-brain? There's no dragon here!

Sir Codsbrain No – but there might be one along in a minute.

Amanda	You what?
	Sir Codsbrain stares out into the audience and waves his sword about.
Sir Codsbrain	Keep off you dragons! Codsbrain's here!
	He puts down his sword and smooches up to Amanda. He thinks he is irresistable.
Sir Codsbrain	Don't worry, luscious lips, you'll be safe with me!
Amanda	(*In disgust*) Keep away from me, you repulsive maggot!
	Amanda whacks Sir Codsbrain in the stomach with her basket. Sir Codsbrain doubles up with pain, but doesn't give up.
Sir Codsbrain	(*In pain*) Ooough! (*Recovering himself*) You're just playing hard to get! Come here, my lovely and I'll give you a knight to remember!
	Sir Codsbrain swoops Amanda up in his arms. She screams and struggles.
Wife of Bath	(*Loudly*) However… (*Sir Codsbrain freezes with Amanda in his arms*) … just at that moment, along came King Arthur – and Queen Guinevere!
	There is a musical fanfare. Queen Guinevere sweeps on stage from behind the booth and instantly takes control.
Guinevere	Put that maiden down, Sir Codsbrain!
	She picks up Sir Codsbrain's sword and threatens him.
Guinevere	(*Expecting to be obeyed*) Put that maiden down!
	Sir Codsbrain lets go of Amanda. Guinevere holds him at sword point.
Guinevere	Where's Arthur? (*Shouting*) Arthur!

King Arthur is lost behind the booth curtain. He flaps it about for a moment before he finds a gap. He dodders down to join the others.

Arthur   Here, my love! (*Seeing* **Sir Codsbrain** *looking embarrassed*) What's up, Codders?

Guinevere   (*To Arthur*) What's the punishment for rescuing a maiden against her will?

Arthur   (*Dithering*) Let me see, er, decapi – you know – severing the brains from the spinal thingamy…

Guinevere   (*Forcefully interrupting*) Yes, yes – never mind all that! Let's just chop his head off!

Sir Codsbrain   (*Begging pitifully to Arthur*) Sire!

Arthur   (*Trying to talk Guinevere round*) Seems a bit steep, dear – eh, what!

Guinevere   Where's the executioner?

Sir Codsbrain looks at Arthur in desperation.

Guinevere   (*Shouting*) Executioner!

Arthur   (*Doing his best to save Sir Codsbrain*) I think it might be his day off, dear.

Amanda   (*Brightly*) I'll do it!

Amanda takes a black hood from her basket, puts it on and becomes the executioner.

Guinevere   (*With enthusiastic approval*) Jolly good show! Done this sort of thing before have you, gal? (*Amanda shakes her head*) Never mind – soon get the hang of it!

Guinevere hands Amanda Sir Codsbrain's sword. She then forces Sir Codsbrain to his *knees. The basket is put in place as an improvised chopping block. **Amanda** wields the sword.*

Guinevere (*To Arthur*) Where's your handkerchief?

Arthur (*Dithering as he searches his clothes*) What? Oh yes, I know it's somewhere…

Guinevere (*To Arthur*) Come here, you old fool!

Guinevere grabs Arthur and pulls a handkerchief out of his sleeve. It is far from clean.

Guinevere Eugh!

She thrusts the dirty handkerchief into Arthur's hand and then turns to speak to Amanda.

Guinevere (*With exaggerated sarcasm*) When his majesty – the king of all England – drops his handkerchief, you chop his head off.

Arthur (*Worried*) Chop my head off?

Guinevere (*Pointing to Sir Codsbrain*) His head! His head! (*To Amanda*) Understand?

Amanda nods.

Sir Codsbrain Your majesty…

Guinevere Shut up! (*To the Wife of Bath*) Ready!

Wife of Bath The king's executioner swings her razor sharp sword in the bright summer's air. (***Amanda** raises the sword over her head*) A carrion crow watches from a tree – waits for a meal of man's flesh! The drums roll. (*There is a quietly intense drum roll*) Arthur drops his handkerchief.

*The **Wife of Bath** rings a bell. **Amanda** starts to bring the sword down.*

Guinevere	(*Interrupting*) Just a moment!

> *Startled, **Amanda** deflects the sword at the last moment and it hits the floor near Sir Codsbrain's head.*

Arthur	What's going on?
Wife of Bath	It's the interval!
Sir Codsbrain	(*Raising his head*) Thank God for that!

> ***Amanda** takes off the black hood, waves to the audience and starts to leave the stage. **Sir Codsbrain** follows her off.*

Sir Codsbrain	(*To Amanda, trying it on*) I say, fancy a drink, gorgeous? I know a quiet little place just near here.

> ***Sir Codsbrain** could suggest the name of a well-known pub close to where this performance takes place.*

Amanda	Go away!
Sir Codsbrain	Don't be like that – I mean, be fair – give a chap a break!
Guinevere	Codsbrain! (*He does not reply*) I'll give him a break! (*To Arthur*) Arthur! Assume the position!

> ***Arthur** bends at the knees in order to give Guinevere a piggy-back. She jumps up on his back.*

Guinevere	Tally-ho!

> ***Arthur** 'gallops' off stage with **Guinevere** on his back.*

Guinevere	(*Calling as they exit*) Codsbrain! Cods-brain!
Wife of Bath	(*To the audience*) Ladies and gentlemen. There will now follow a short interval, after which we'll all return – to see Sir Codsbrain get his head chopped off!

The Wife of Bath leaves her pulpit, takes a bow and exits. The Alchemists and the cast lead the audience in applause. Geoffrey is then taken off by the Alchemists for intravenous tea and biscuits. Interval.

Introduction to Part Two

There is the sound of whistles, cheers, and percussion instruments as part two begins. Jocasta and Michelangelo leap onto the stage to greet the audience.

Jocasta	Ladies and gentlemen! Welcome back to part two of The Canterbury Tales.
Michelangelo	We hope you enjoyed the interval!
Jocasta	Welcome back also to our honoured guest...
Michelangelo	... half-dead, half-alive, but full of quiet charm.
Jocasta	The man who once wrote of himself, 'Thy drasty rymyng is nat worth a toord'! The ever popular...
Jocasta ⎫ Michelangelo ⎭	... Geoffrey Chaucer!

There are more whistles and cheers as Amelia and Giovanni bring Geoffrey on stage to receive the audience's applause. Then, they prop him against the stage left side of the booth.

The Wife of Bath's Tale (Part Two)

There is a fanfare. The Alchemists leave as the Wife of Bath enters and goes to her pulpit. Sir Codsbrain enters, pushed on by Amanda and Guinevere. Amanda carries Sir Codsbrain's sword and a black hood. Arthur tags along behind. They take up the positions they were in when Sir Codsbrain's execution was interrupted. Sir Codsbrain whimpers as Guinevere forces him to his knees.

Guinevere   (*To Sir Codsbrain*) Kneel! Not a word!

Guinevere pushes Sir Codsbrain's head on the basket handle, facing the audience.

Arthur   (*To Guinevere*) My dear – I really don't think…

Guinevere   How true! (*To Amanda*) Ready, executioner?

Amanda nods. She puts on her black hood.

Guinevere   (*To the Wife of Bath*) Ready!

Wife of Bath   The king's executioner swings her razor sharp sword in the bright summer's air. (*Amanda raises the sword over her head*) A carrion crow watches from a tree – waits for a meal of man's flesh. The drums roll. (*There is a quietly intense drum roll*) Arthur drops his handkerchief.

Amanda starts to bring the sword down.

Guinevere   (*Interrupting*) Just a moment!

Startled, Amanda deflects the sword at the last moment, and it hits the floor near Sir Codsbrain's head. The shock makes him thrust his head into the basket. Sir Codsbrain freezes in that position.

Arthur   What's going on?

Guinevere	I've changed my mind!
Arthur	What?
Guinevere	It's a shame to kill him. It's a waste of a knight.
Arthur	It's only Codders, dear…

Sir Codsbrain remains kneeling. Amanda takes off the black hood and walks around him.

Amanda	There's nothing wrong with his body! It's his brain that's useless.
Arthur	(*Still trying to work out Guinevere's bad pun*) Oh, I see – 'waste of a night'!
Guinevere	(*Looking at Arthur in disgust*) Completely useless! (*To the audience*) Most of you men here have the same problem!
Arthur	What about the execution?
Guinevere	It's postponed! Instead I'm going to find out if it's possible for a man to be re-educated!

She takes the sword from Amanda and slaps Sir Codsbrain on his buttocks with the flat of the blade.

Guinevere	Sir Codsbrain!

Sir Codsbrain jumps to his feet, with his head still in the basket.

Sir Codsbrain	By the bunion of Saint Blaise! – I'm still alive! (*He takes off the basket and puts it down*) It's a miracle! (*To the women in the audience*) Hey girls, how would you like a man with miraculous powers?
Guinevere	Codsbrain! You are still under sentence of death!

She passes the sword to Amanda.

Sir Codsbrain	(*Backing away from Guinevere*) Didn't mean it. Sorry! Sorry! I'll be good!

Amanda moves behind Sir Codsbrain and lifts the sword up between his legs.

Amanda	(*To Guinevere*) Let's chop it off!

Sir Codsbrain *wrings his hands.*

Sir Codsbrain	(*Begging and pleading*) Spare me, oh queen! Spare me!

Amanda raises the sword above her head again. **Sir Codsbrain** *falls to his knees, trembling.*

Guinevere	(*To Amanda*) Not yet! (*To Sir Codsbrain*) Listen, worm – if you can return here in one year's time and answer a special test question – I will spare your life.

Sir Codsbrain	(*Over-excited*) Yes! Yes! I'll do it! (*He gets up and starts to leave*) I'll find the answer! I'll return with the answer!(*He comes back*) What's the question?

Guinevere	A question, Codsbrain, that has never crossed your mind before – 'What is it that women most desire'?

Arthur	I've no idea!

Guinevere	Nobody asked you, you old fool! Go off and play with your round table!

Arthur dodders off stage, calling as he goes.

Arthur	Merlin! Mer-lin!

Guinevere	(*To Amanda*) What about you?

Amanda curtsies and passes the sword to **Guinevere.** *She picks up her basket.*

Amanda	I'm going to take this basket of raspberries to my dear old grandmother who lives in a little house in the woods.

	Amanda skips off stage. **Guinevere** *stands bemused for a moment.* **Sir Codsbrain** *goes to follow Amanda.*
Guinevere	(*To Sir Codsbrain*) What do you think you're up to?
Sir Codsbrain	(*Starting guiltily*) Oh yes, right – erm, er, excuse me, your majesty, what was that question again?
	Guinevere *roars and brandishes the sword at him.*
Sir Codsbrain	(*Quickly*) Oh yes, oh yes! I remember!
	Guinevere *shoves the sword into* **Sir Codsbrain's** *hands, gives him a look of withering contempt and exits.* **Sir Codsbrain** *shares his thoughts with the audience.*
Sir Codsbrain	(*Thinking aloud*) 'What is it that women most desire?' (*Suddenly inspired*) Well, it's obvious really, isn't it? What they most desire is me!
	The audience, encouraged by the cast, react negatively to this statement. The **Wife of Bath** *gives Sir Codsbrain a look of stern disapproval.*
Sir Codsbrain	(*Realizing his mistake*) No, there's got to be more to it than that. The real question is, 'What do women most desire apart from me?'. Should be easy enough to find out!
Wife of Bath	And so Sir Codsbrain went off to ask women what they most desired. It wasn't as easy as he thought.
	Sir Codsbrain *goes into the audience and asks a number of women what they most desire. This improvisation continues until the* **Wife of Bath** *interrupts and* **Sir Codsbrain** *returns to the stage.*
Wife of Bath	The weeks went by. The months went by. Most women refused to answer his question.

*In the following sequence, the **Wife of Bath** leaves the stage left pulpit and becomes all the different women visited by Sir Codsbrain. Both actors move about the stage and mime the actions as they are described.*

Wife of Bath   They slammed the door on his foot.

Sir Codsbrain   Yeoww!

Wife of Bath   Smashed the door on his nose.

Sir Codsbrain   Yeargh!

Wife of Bath   Poked him in the eye with a spindle.

Sir Codsbrain   Owwww!

Wife of Bath   Slapped him round the face with a wet fish, emptied a pisspot on his head…

Sir Codsbrain   Yuchchch!

Wife of Bath   …and told him to go back to Camelot and get himself decapitated.

*The **Wife of Bath** returns to the stage left pulpit. **Sir Codsbrain** sits on a bench and sings sadly to the tune of 'Greensleeves'.*

Sir Codsbrain   Alas! Alas! O Woe! Alack! To Camelot I must go back! To Camelot I must go back! Alas! O Woe! Alack!

Wife of Bath   Slowly and sadly Sir Codsbrain journeyed back to Camelot to get his head cut off. You may ask why he didn't run off to France or Flanders or the magic land of Whipperginney.

Sir Codsbrain   (*Standing up proudly*) Because I am a Knight of the Round Table, and bound by my honour never, never to run away.

Wife of Bath   Because he was too stupid! However, as he plodded his weary way along the road to Camelot, he happened to pass a wood.

Sir Codsbrain	A wood!
Wife of Bath	From out of the wood came beautiful music.

> *Beautiful music is played. This could be medieval dance music or something simple on a glockenspiel.*

Sir Codsbrain	(*Responding to the music*) That's – beautiful!
Wife of Bath	Codsbrain followed the sound through the trees until he saw a wondrous sight.

> *Sir Codsbrain moves across the stage as if he is following a vision which only he can see.*

Wife of Bath	There, on a green in the wood…
Sir Codsbrain	Four and twenty beautiful ladies.
Wife of Bath	Dancing.
Sir Codsbrain	Enchanting!
Wife of Bath	Twelve.
Sir Codsbrain	(*Puzzled as the ladies begin to vanish before his eyes*) Eight.
Wife of Bath	Six.
Sir Codsbrain	Four.
Wife of Bath	Three.
Sir Codsbrain	Two.

> *The **Wife of Bath** leaves the stage left pulpit and opens the booth curtains to reveal an old woman with her back turned. The **old woman** spins round. A half-mask gives her the appearance of an ugly, frightening crone.*

Old Woman	One!

*Sir Codsbrain turns to face the old woman. He gasps. The music stops suddenly. The **Wife of Bath** returns to her stage left pulpit. Sir Codsbrain backs away from the old woman.*

Old Woman (*Leaving the booth and approaching Sir Codsbrain*) Lost your way, young man? Never mind! You might be glad you missed your path! You might have done yourself a good turn! We old women know a lot of things!

Sir Codsbrain Really! Well I'm a dead man if I don't find out what women most desire.

Old Woman Easy!

Sir Codsbrain Easy! If you could tell me the answer, I'd pay you well! You could have anything you wanted! Gold, silver…

Old Woman (*Interrupting*) I don't want your wealth. I just want you to promise me that you'll do whatever I ask of you, if it is in your power.

Sir Codsbrain (*Going down on one knee*) I promise! On my honour as a knight! (*Leaping to his feet and waving his sword*) What do you want me to do? Kill a few dragons?

Old Woman Later. First we must go to Camelot.

Sir Codsbrain But what's the answer to the queen's question?

Old Woman There are many answers that can be right.

Sir Codsbrain (*Impatiently*) I know. I know!

Old Woman But here is an answer that none of the ladies dare say is wrong. Listen closely.

*The **old woman** beckons Sir Codsbrain. As he gets closer, he realizes she stinks. He reacts, hesitates, but has to go nearer because he is desperate. There is a musical trill as the **old woman** whispers in Sir Codsbrain's ear.*

Wife of Bath	As soon as he heard what the old woman had to say, Sir Codsbrain stopped looking so miserable.
Sir Codsbrain	(*Happy and excited*) Huzzah! Huzzah! (*To the old woman*) Sit on the back of my horse! It's time to return to Camelot!
	There is the sound of coconut shell horses hooves. **Sir Codsbrain** *and the* **old woman** *'gallop' into the audience. At the same time, the whole cast sing, well over-the-top, in the style of a big, stage musical.*
Cast	Camelot! Camelot! Camelo-o-o-ot!
	The **Wife of Bath** *leaves her pulpit to close the booth curtains.* **Arthur, Guinevere** *and* **Amanda** *enter to take up their positions at the court of Camelot.*
Wife of Bath	(*As she returns to her pulpit*) Camelot was full of people who had come to hear Sir Codsbrain's answer – and watch his head fall off! (*She looks around the audience*) There were knaves and rogues, knights and maidens, noble ladies and wise widows, King Arthur…
Arthur	… and Queen Guinevere!
Guinevere	Where's that Codsbrain? He's too stupid to run away!
Sir Codsbrain	(*Coming on stage from the audience*) Here, your majesty… (*He kneels and presents his sword*) …on my honour as a knight!
Guinevere	(*Taking Sir Codsbrain's sword and threatening him*) Codsbrain – you've had a year. Tell us the answer to my question right now or we'll chop your head off!
Sir Codsbrain	(*To the court and the audience*) What women most desire, basically, in general, er… (*losing confidence*) …taking all the factors into account…
Arthur	Come on, Codders – spit it out!
Guinevere	Hurry up or you're headless!

Sir Codsbrain	(*As if he's learned the words by heart*) What women most desire is to have dominion and power over their husbands, or over their lovers. (*To all the women on stage and in the audience*) You want the mastery! Who will contradict me?
Wife of Bath	There was a moment's silence. There was none who would say that he was completely right.
Old Woman	(*Cackling to herself in the audience*) But none that would say that he was wrong.
Guinevere	Codsbrain… (*She raises the sword as if she is about to chop his head off, but instead touches him on the shoulder with the flat of the blade*) …you have won your life.
Sir Codsbrain	(*Leaping about*) Huzzah! Huzzah!
Guinevere	But I can't understand how a dim-witted chauvinist like you could have thought up an answer like that!
Sir Codsbrain	It was simplicity itself!

*The **old woman** hobbles furiously on stage from the audience.*

Old Woman	(*To Sir Codsbrain*) Liar! (*To the others*) I told him the answer! And what is more, he said that he would do the first thing I asked of him in return!

*The stink of the old woman hits Arthur. He makes a face and steps back. **Guinevere** also reacts to the smell. Then, she recovers herself.*

Guinevere	Aha! It all makes sense! (*With relish*) What do you ask of him?
Old Woman	(*Gleefully*) I ask that he marry me! I saved his life! And now I demand that he make me his wife!
Sir Codsbrain	Oh no! Oh woe!
Guinevere	Wonderful!
Amanda	Excellent!

Arthur	How terribly romantic!
Guinevere	You must be married at once!
Arthur	A priest! We need a priest! Why is there never a priest around when you want one?

> *The **Wife of Bath** leaves her pulpit and finds a member of the audience to be the priest.*

Wife of Bath	(*Picking on someone*) You! You're a priest! Don't argue! Father, what's your name?

> *The person playing the priest is encouraged to give a name.*

Guinevere	Oh yes, Father … (*Use the name given by the member of the audience*)

> *The **Wife of Bath** brings the **priest** onto the stage, and then returns to her pulpit.*

Guinevere	(*To Amanda*) Give him a hand, gal!

> *Amanda dresses the **priest** in a mitre and stole from the coatstand. Then, she gives him a prayer card with the necessary lines of script written on it and puts him in position, facing the audience.*

Guinevere	(*To the priest*) That's right! Get some proper kit on! Just the ticket! (*She glares at Sir Codsbrain and speaks again to the priest*) Don't hang about or he'll slip the net!
Arthur	(*To the audience*) Quiet please! We're going to have a marriage! (*To the priest*) Are you ready?

> *Arthur nods to the **Wife of Bath** who conducts the audience and cast in a version of 'Here Comes the Bride'.*

All	Der dum der dum! Der dum der dum! Der dum der der dum der der dum der dum!

*The **old woman** kneels down before the priest. **Sir Codsbrain** is forced to his knees by **Amanda** and **Guinevere**.*

Priest (*Reading from the card*) Do you old, poor, smelly, ugly woman take Sir Codsbrain to be your lawful wedded husband?

Old Woman I do!

Priest (*Reading from the card*) Do you Sir Codsbrain take this woman to be your lawful wedded wife?

Sir Codsbrain Do I have to?

Guinevere (*Shouting*) Executioner!

Sir Codsbrain (*Hurriedly*) I do. I do. I do!

Priest (*Reading from the card*) I now pronounce you man and wife.

Arthur Is that it?

Guinevere That's the marriage over, and now I think we should leave them alone together!

***Amanda** removes the priest's mitre and stole, hangs them up, and sends him back to the audience.*

Guinevere Thank you, Father! Thank you, everyone!

Arthur Carry on, Codders!

***Guinevere** bends her knees, ready to give Arthur a piggy-back.*

Guinevere Come on, Arthur! Jump aboard!

***Arthur** jumps up on Guinevere's back.*

Guinevere Tally-ho!

The cast lead the audience in applause.
Guinevere *and* ***Arthur*** *start to exit.*
Amanda *follows them, opening the side and front curtains of the booth as she goes. A large quilt covers the floor of the booth. It looks like an extremely big, four poster bed.* ***Guinevere*** *pauses for a moment as she leaves the stage.* ***Arthur*** *shouts back to Sir Codsbrain.*

Arthur　　Good luck, Codders!

Sir Codsbrain gives him a hang-dog look.

Arthur　　(*Cheerfully*) I should use a clothes peg!

Slushy, romantic music is played as the old woman quickly gets into the bed and sits up with the quilt around her. ***Sir Codsbrain*** *gets up and fiddles about with his clothes downstage of the booth. Instead of taking off his tabard, he wraps the ends between his legs and round his waist and knots them.*

Old Woman　　(*Eventually*) What's the problem, loverboy?

Sir Codsbrain　　There are several problems, my beloved!

Old Woman　　Such as?

Sir Codsbrain　　You're old. You're poor. You're smelly and ugly!

Old Woman　　Is that all?

Sir Codsbrain　　It's enough!

The ***old woman*** *gets out of the bed and marches towards Sir Codsbrain.*

Old Woman　　Now you listen to me, mister big mouth, empty-headed, fat-faced, Sir Knight Codsbrain! It's about time you learned a few things.

Sir Codsbrain　　How dare you...

Old Woman	(*Interrupting*) Shut up! Number one – I may be poor and of humble birth, but is poverty a crime? You call yourself a Christian knight – was Jesus rich?
Sir Codsbrain	Well that's different...
Old Woman	Number two – I may be old, so where is your respect for age Sir Rude-Tongued Knight?
Sir Codsbrain	I say!
Old Woman	Number three – I may be smelly, but there's been no regular hot water since the Romans left! You smell pretty disgusting yourself!
Sir Codsbrain	I'm a man!
Old Woman	You're a smelly man! Number four – I may be ugly. I may even be old, poor, smelly, and ugly – but I'm not likely to go running off with some other knight, am I? It's your decision!
Sir Codsbrain	What decision?
Old Woman	Listen dimwit – do you want me as I am before you, to be your true and faithful wife? Or do you want a beautiful, young bimbo and a house full of knights coming round to chat me up every day? You choose!

*The **old woman** returns to the booth.*

Sir Codsbrain	I, er, um, er, um...
Wife of Bath	It was too much for Codsbrain's brain. His thoughts bounced about in his head!
Sir Codsbrain	Um, er, um, er...
Wife of Bath	Finally, he said something he had never said in his life before.
Sir Codsbrain	I don't know.

Sir Codsbrain joins the old woman in the booth.

Wife of Bath	And then Sir Codsbrain said something else he had never said in his life before.
Sir Codsbrain	You decide. (*He kneels*) My lady and my love. I leave it entirely up to you. You are the wisest, you decide what is best for us both.
Old Woman	And so I have the mastery over you?
Sir Codsbrain	Yes. Certainly. I think it's best!
Old Woman	In that case, come and kiss me. No more quarrel between us two.

> *Sir Codsbrain and the old woman embrace. There is music as the old woman turns away from the audience, takes off her half-mask, and is transformed into a beautiful girl. The music stops as she turns back to the audience.*

Old Woman	I will be both beautiful, and good and true!
Wife of Bath	(*Leaving her pulpit to close the curtains of the booth*) And all at once they dived into bed, to kiss and kiss a thousand times, and live happily together ever after – well, a few months at least! (*Walking downstage to address the audience*) And may God send us husbands meek, young and lively in bed, and give us grace to outlive those we marry. And send chauvinist males to an early grave. And may all bad-tempered, mean, old skinflint misers – catch the plague!

Interlude

> *The **Wife of Bath** takes a bow and the cast and audience applaud. As she leaves the stage, she blows Geoffrey a kiss. The **Alchemists** rush over to see how he is.*

Michelangelo	Geoffrey!
Giovanni	He twitched.

Jocasta	He liked that one!
Giovanni	More romance, more action, something quick and slick!
Amelia	The Knight's Tale!
Michelangelo	Takes forever!
Amelia	Not the way we do it!

The Knight's Tale

*Amelia blows a whistle which is the signal for a troop of mummers to march on stage. The **Knight** leads, followed by **Theseus**, **Emily**, **Palamon**, **Arcite**, and the gods – **Venus**, **Mars**, and **Diana**. They are accompanied by pipes, drums, bells, tabors, perhaps a squeeze box and other noise-makers such as chains, rattles and thunderboard. They all wear mumming style costumes and carry props such as kitchen utensils (weapons), mops and buckets (for jousting), a stool (a throne), things to use as a disguise.*

*As the mummers arrive, the **Alchemists** start to re-arrange the set, moving the table and one of the benches stage right (making a stage right extension to the booth with the bench as a step). The other bench is moved further stage left. The **Alchemists** then exit.*

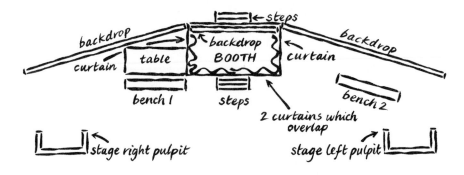

The mummers stand in a large semi-circle facing the audience. They perform in a traditional mumming way, stepping forward to speak and returning to their place when not performing. There is a bang on a drum. The mummers sit down except for the **Knight,** *who steps forward into the stage left pulpit.*

Knight   My reputation speaks for itself. I've fought in the king's service all over the world – Alexandria, Prussia, Russia, Granada, Turkey! I don't go for fancy clothes, just my coarse tunic and rusty chain mail. I'm a man of action not of words, but if you would like to hear a plain story of chivalry and romance – listen to this.

He rings the story bell as **Theseus** *rises and steps forward.*

Theseus   In comes I Theseus. In days gone by
The noble Duke of Athens am I.

There is the sound of chimes as **Emily** *rises and steps forward.*

Emily   And I so beautiful and fair to see
I am his wife's sister. I am Emily!

Emily *returns to sit in the semi-circle.*

Theseus   The King of Thebes, I beat in bloody war.
And after on the field, wounded full sore,
Palamon and Arcite, brave knights of Thebes, I found
And now in Athens prison keep them bound!

Theseus *returns to sit in the semi-circle.*
Palamon *rises and steps forward.*

Palamon   Here am I Palamon! I shed a bitter tear!
For I must spend my life in this gloomy prison here!

There is a shaking of chains to create a prison atmosphere. **Arcite** *(pronounced Ah-see-tea) rises and steps forward to join Palamon.*

Arcite	I am Arcite. A bitter tear shed I! For I must stay, with him, in prison, till I die!

There is more shaking of chains.

Palamon	O woe! Alas! O misery!
Arcite	We two never shall be free.
Palamon	Poor Palamon.
Arcite	And Arcite.

Emily stands and walks downstage to sit by herself.

Palamon	But wait! Look through the window! Lo! There walks a goddess on this earth below, With yellow hair, come down from heaven above. I give her my heart, at once, and all my love.
Arcite	That is no goddess! That is Emily, Sister-in-law of Theseus, that's who we see! She walks in the garden at dawn to honour the spring! I give her my love! She makes my glad heart sing!
Palamon	Look not on her! My eyes were first to see!
Arcite	You saw a goddess. I saw Emily.
Palamon	I saw her first.
Arcite	All's fair in love and war.
Palamon	We're locked in prison.
Arcite	What are we fighting for?

Theseus rises and steps forward.

Theseus	Here ye! Here ye! In comes I Theseus to say Arcite shall be freed from prison on this day But if you walk again into my land I'll have to cut your head off! Understand?

Theseus returns to his place.

Arcite   (*To Palamon*) O woe! O woe! It's better in than out!

Palamon   I don't see what you've got to moan about!

Arcite   I leave the prison, yes, and this country!
Never again will I see Emily!

Arcite returns to the semi-circle.

Knight   (*To the audience*) Now which of these two knights feels the
most pain?
Palamon sees his love again and again
Though from a prison cell, but Arcite
Can never see his love though he walks free!

Palamon returns to his seat in the semi-circle. Theseus sits on a throne (a wooden stool) beside Emily. Arcite steps forward in 'disguise' (a false beard?) with a fly-whisk (spatula?).

Arcite   Back comes I Arcite, wearing a disguise
As a servant and page I appear to Theseus's eyes!
I fan his face and brush the flies away
And now I can look on Emily every day!

Palamon rises and moves downstage right.

Palamon   Hold hard! Here am I, Palamon, behind this tree!

Arcite crosses to Palamon.

Arcite   I thought you were in prison.

Palamon   No, I'm free.
I have escaped my jail this very night
And now for the love of Emily we'll fight!

*Palamon and Arcite pick up 'weapons'.
They start to fight in a stylized manner.*

Palamon   Ouch! Oooo! Aaah!

Arcite	Aaaah Oooo! Ouch!

Theseus rises and interrupts them.

Theseus	Here comes I Theseus in a terrible rage To find an escaped prisoner fighting with my page!

Arcite and Palamon fall to their knees.

Arcite	My noble Lord, you may chop off my head, But I have things to say which must be said. I am Arcite that you did set free, Returned in disguise for love of Emily!

Palamon	I'm in love with her too. I love her more than you.

Theseus	My heart is touched. Your freedoms, I restore.

Emily	(*To the world in general*) I've never seen this pair of twerps before!

Theseus	We'll have a proper joust on Saturday! The winner can marry Emily straight away!

Emily	Thanks for nothing!

Theseus	(*Trying to soothe her*) Gracious Emily!

Emily	Thanks for nothing! Nobody asked me!

They all return to their seats in the semi-circle.

Knight	Then early the next morning, in the early morning light They each went to a temple to pray before the fight!

The gods: Venus, Mars and Diana, rise and step forward. They stand like statues in a temple. Palamon comes to pray first. He falls on his knees before Venus.

Palamon	O Venus, in your half shell, sailing on the sea. Hear my prayer and give to me the love of Emily.

Venus	What you wish is what shall be!

Palamon returns to his seat. Arcite falls on his knees before Mars.

Arcite	O Mars, red god of war, in armour bright. Grant to me the victory in the fight.
Mars	To do your will is my delight!

Arcite returns to his seat. Emily approaches Diana.

Emily	O Diana, huntress free and strong To neither of these knights would I belong. But if I marry must, I pray to you, Let me marry the one that loves me true!
Diana	Just as you ask so shall I do!

Emily and the gods return to their seats. There is music as the mumming troop prepare for the jousting contest. Mops can be used as lances and metal colanders or buckets as helmets. Palamon and Arcite, wearing their 'helmets' and carrying 'lances' go to opposite sides of the stage. Theseus steps forward; the music stops.

Theseus	Palamon and Arcite, the time has come. Now fight together till the fight is done! One!

Palamon and Arcite charge at each other across the stage – and miss.

Theseus	Two!

They charge at each other again – and miss.

Theseus	A final three!

They charge for a third time. Arcite hits Palamon, who falls to the ground.

Arcite	Oh, thank you, Mars! The victory falls to me!

The mummers create a crash of thunder.

Arcite	Oh no! A thunderbolt falls from the sky! (*He falls down*) I fall from off my horse! I'm hurt! I die!

*Theseus walks between the fallen Palamon
and Arcite.*

Theseus	There, in the sea of sorrow's deepest part, There is the place at which the cure should start! (*Pointing to Arcite*) Mars gave him victory but now he's dead. It's Palamon now who must our Emily wed!

Palamon	Oh thank you, Venus! My heart's wish come true! (*To Emily*) I never wanted victory – only you!

Emily rises and steps forward.

Emily	Thanks to Diana! I prefer the knight Who thinks the prize is worth more than the fight!
Knight	And so they were married and my tale is done! I think you will agree that the best men, and women, won!

Interlude

*All the mummers return to the semi-circle,
stand and bow. There is applause, led by the
cast. The mummers, led by the **Knight**, exit,
accompanied by music, just as they entered.
They take their props with them. As they
leave the stage, one of the mummers pulls a
string of joke sausages out of Geoffrey's belly
and dances off with them. The **Alchemists**
rush to take a look at Geoffrey.*

Jocasta	(*Calling after the mummers*) Hey! Watch what you're doing!
Amelia	What happened?
	Michelangelo takes Geoffrey's pulse.
Giovanni	Has he come to life?
Michelangelo	(*Looking into Geoffrey's eyes*) He's more dead than ever!
Jocasta	No time left. We'll have to use shock treatment!
	*The **Alchemists** look at each other, in horror.*
Alchemists	The Miller's Tale!
Michelangelo	Told by...
Alchemists	...the Miller!

*On hearing his name, the **Miller** staggers on stage. He is quite drunk, and carries a bottle in one hand and a sack of flour in the other. He starts arguing with the **Alchemists** as they leave to watch from the side of the stage.*

The Miller's Tale

Miller	(*To the Alchemists*) Where do you think you're going, eh? What's goin' on here?

He sees the audience, and releases a series of burps and belches.

Miller	(*To the audience, aggressively*) It's a lie! As the devil is my witness, I never robbed anyone of any flour! (*He opens his hands wide*) I never... (*He sees the bag of flour in his own hand, tries to hide it, but then decides to go on the attack*) You clever students with your clever ideas! I'll break all the bones in your bodies, by Christ's arms and blood! Hic! (*Suddenly apologetic*) Sorry about the bad language. I've had a few bottles at the inn and I'm – what's the word? Can't think of it! Oh yes – drunk! (*Suddenly aggressive again*) But I'm not pissed! By the hairs on the wart on my nose, I'll break every bone in – (*He becomes confused*) Oh yes, I've said that already haven't I? (*Friendly*) I know, how would you like to hear a story?

*As he speaks he moves to open the front curtains of the booth, revealing **Alison** and **John**, in a posed tableau.*

Miller	It's very rude and very lewd. (*He burps*) You'll love it!

*The **Miller** staggers to the stage right pulpit where he drops his sack of flour.*

Miller	Once upon a time... (*He rings the story bell furiously and shouts at the audience*) Shush, will yer! I'm telling a story! Once upon a ... you know...

Alison is fed up of waiting. As she comes down from the booth, she addresses the audience.

Alison	Once upon a time, there lived in Oxford a rich, miserly, boring, old carpenter, called John.
Miller	What a boring name!
John	Boring – but rich.

Alison	Yeah. So he paid my parents a load of money and I had to marry him.

***Alison** marches back to the booth to join John.*

John	Alison, my beautiful young wife! You've got a body like a polecat – or is it a stoat? No, a weasel, that's it, a body like a weasel.
Alison	The wedding night was a nightmare.
John	I had a bad back and a headache.
Alison	And the next night!
John	And the night after that!
Miller	He dressed her in fine clothes and sat her in his house to look pretty. What a waste.

*As **John** talks to Alison, her body language shows how bored she is.*

John	I had this wood-carving knife, you know, Alison, when I were a lad. It had a lovely rosewood handle – or were it briar – good workmanship, can't get 'em nowadays – and all I'd do, all day long, was sit on the step all day and whittle – whittle, whittle, whittle – all day long, whittle, whittle…
Alison	(*Exploding to the audience*) I'm bored out of my mind!

***Nicholas** enters and climbs onto the table.*

Nicholas	But there was a tiny room upstairs which John had rented, at a huge price, to a handsome young student – me, Nicholas!
Miller	A lazy, good for nothing art student.
Nicholas	My art is my life.
Miller	Yeuch!

Alison	Poor Nicholas didn't have a girlfriend. He spent all day on his own.
Miller	Playing with his astrolabe!
John	(*Leaving the booth and standing to one side*) One day, while I was away on business…
Miller	… Nicholas ran downstairs…

Nicholas runs from the table into the booth.

Nicholas	… and grabbed Alison firmly… (*He does so*)
Alison	…in a private place…
Miller	… the kitchen! Alison made a loud scream.
Alison	Eeeek!
Nicholas	Alison! Have mercy!
Alison	Nicholas! (*To the audience*) I've had my eye on him!
Nicholas	Make love with me now!
Alison	I dare not! John is so jealous! What if he discovered us!
Nicholas	Don't worry! I have a plan!

Nicholas runs back to the table where he sits and meditates.

Miller	But Nicholas wasn't the only one to have a plan. Nicholas wasn't the only admirer of the beautiful Alison.
Alison	My other admirer was…

Absolon enters, stage left, below the booth.

Absolon	Me! Absolon. The parish clerk.
Alison	He couldn't take his eyes off me!

Absolon	I had a plan as well.

Absolon and *Alison* *perform a series of mimes during the following sequence.*

Absolon	I gave her chocolates.
Alison	Thank you!
Absolon	Flowers!
Alison	Thank you!
Absolon	Poems – Roses are red. Violets are blue. You are so sweet…
Alison	Get lost! Thank you.
Absolon	Money!
Alison	Thank you so much.
Absolon	I came to sing outside her window! (*Singing dreadfully*) O Alison! I love you true! I'd like a little kiss from you! La la la la la la la!
Alison	Buzz off!

Absolon *slumps sadly over to the stage left bench.*

Miller	It was a useless plan.
Alison	I was more interested in Nicholas.
Nicholas	And I had an ingenious plan.
All	Nicholas and his ingenious plan.

Nicholas *stands on the table, transfixed, hands uplifted, as though he is seeing a vision.* *John* *climbs back into the booth.*

John	One day, I came back from business to find that Nicholas had been locked in his room for days.
Alison	(*To John*) Nicholas! Nicholas! He's been locked in his room for days!
John	Break down the door!

> *John* and *Alison* mime breaking down the door, accompanied by percussion sound effects. They crash onto the table, down the bench step, and onto the stage.

Alison	When we broke down the door to Nicholas's room we found him standing in a trance.
Nicholas	(*Eyes glazed, as if speaking on the telephone*) Yes – yes, all right – yes, fine – yes, I'll tell him – bye! (*Suddenly alert, he speaks urgently*) I've been speaking with God.

> *John* gasps and *Alison* pretends to be shocked.

Nicholas	And God says that there's going to be another flood.
John	Oh no! Oh woe! We'll all be drowned!
Nicholas	Not so!

> *Nicholas* steps down off the table and takes *John* by his hands.

Nicholas	God says that we shall be saved! God says that you must saw some big wooden butter tubs in half with your sacred hands, and hang them in the loft.

> As he speaks, *Nicholas* walks excitedly around the stage, followed by *Alison* and *John*.

Nicholas	Tonight we will sleep in the wooden tubs. When the flood comes – we cut the ropes holding the butter tubs, drop onto the water and float away safely like little ducks.

Alison	Like little ducks.
John	Like little ducks!
Nicholas	Hooray!
Alison	Hooray!
John	Hooray!

> *Nicholas and Alison laugh, as John goes and gets three tubs. They close the booth curtains. The stand-up bed is assembled.*

Miller   What a load of tripe! By evening John was bent double with pain!

> *John enters hauling three large tubs (waste paper bins or garden tubs).*

John   (*Moaning aloud as he lifts the tubs onto the table*) I've spent all day sawing butter tubs in half – hauling them up to the attic – and hanging them on the rafters!

> *John, Alison and Nicholas climb into the butter tubs. John gets into the tub which is furthest from the booth.*

Miller   The silly old fool crawled into his tub, and settled down to sleep.

Nicholas   Sure of God's special favour.

Alison   Sure that he would be saved from the flood.

John   (*Brandishing an imaginary axe*) I've got a sharp axe ready to cut the rope when the water rises.

> *John settles down to sleep in his tub. Nicholas and Alison do too, enjoying the pretense.*

Nicholas   (*Piously*) Night-night, John! (*Saucily*) Night-night, Alison!

Alison	(*Excitedly*) Night-night, Nicholas! (*Ungraciously*) Night-night, John!

John	(*Innocently*) Night-night, Alison! Night-night, Nicholas!

They all begin to snore.

| Alison
Nicholas } | Zzzzzzzzz! |
| John | |

Alison and Nicholas check that John is asleep. Then they creep out of their tubs and tiptoe into the booth.

Miller	But Nicholas and Alison didn't go to sleep. They crept downstairs and jumped into bed!

Nicholas and Alison giggle from behind the curtain. Absolon gets up from the bench.

Absolon	Oh where are you Alison, my sweet lamb? It is I, Absolon! I can't sleep for thinking of you!

Alison opens the front curtains of the booth. Nicholas is standing between the covers of the stand-up bed. He pops his head down, between the covers, out of sight.

Alison	(*To Absolon*) Get lost you drip! I love another! Buzz off or I'll throw a brick at your head!

Absolon	Just one kiss. Please!

Alison	Will you go away if I give you a kiss?

Absolon	I will!

Alison	Just watch this, Nicholas!

Nicholas sticks his head out above the bed covers.

Miller	Nights were very dark in the early Middle Ages. There were no street lights and no glass in the windows.

> *Alison turns her back and sticks her bottom out of the front of the booth. (A joke shop fake bottom will avoid embarrassment.) Absolon comes downstage to talk to the audience.*

Absolon	What kind of a kiss should I give my love? I know! A big wet sloppy one, a kiss that she will remember forever!

> *Absolon practises some kisses as he approaches Alison.*

Miller	(*To audience as* **Absolon** *prepares himself*) Remember! There hasn't been any decent water supply since the Romans left! There's no toothpaste with stripes either. One part of the body smells just as bad as any other part.

> *Absolon starts to smooch.*

Miller	It was a long passionate kiss. But even while Absolon was smooching and snogging he knew something was not quite right.
Absolon	(*Turning back to the audience*) Funny! I've kissed girls before – but there's something very different about this one.

> *Alison can't contain her giggles any longer.*

Alison	Tee, hee!
Absolon	Oh no! What have I done? Aaaagh!

> *Absolon runs downstage wiping his mouth. Alison jumps back between the covers of the bed with Nicholas. She is giggling fit to burst.*

Alison	He, he! That'll teach him!
Nicholas	(*Mimicking Absolon*) 'There's something very different about this one!'

	Alison and *Nicholas* collapse under the covers with laughter.
Miller	Absolon didn't laugh. He was too busy scrubbing his lips with sand and straw!
Absolon	I don't think I love her any more!
Alison } **Nicholas** }	Tee, hee!
Absolon	(*Coldly furious*) Revenge! I will have revenge!
Miller	Absolon went straight away to see his friend, Gervais – the blacksmith!
	Gervais enters stage left. He carries a metal poker, a mallet and a bench. He creates his blacksmith's shop and starts to hammer the poker on the bench with his mallet. Percussion instruments provide sound effects.
Absolon	I say, Gervais, may I borrow that red hot poker?
Gervais	What do you want with a red hot poker at this time of night?
Absolon	Mind your own business!
Gervais	All right, all right, keep yer hair on.
	He wraps a rag from his pocket around the poker to create a handle and gives it to **Absolon.**
Gervais	(*Warningly*) Mind you don't burn yerself!
Absolon	Don't be stupid. (**Absolon** *does burn himself*) Ow! (*He blows on his fingers*) Thanks, Gervais!
	Absolon takes up a position downstage, far right. *Gervais* exits stage left, taking his bench and mallet with him.

Miller	As you might guess, Absolon ran back to Alison's window with the red hot poker.
Absolon	(*Calling to Alison*) Alison! My love! I've bought you a gold ring! Give me another kiss and it's yours!
Nicholas	He, he! It's my turn this time!
Miller	This time Nicholas jammed his arse in the window frame.

> ***Nicholas*** *gets out of the bed, turns his back, and sticks his bottom out of the front of the booth.*

Absolon	Speak, pretty bird, for I know not where thou art!
Miller	At once Nicholas let fly a fart – as loud as a thunderclap!

> *There is an appropriate sound effect.*

Alison	Absolon was half-blinded by the blast!
Absolon	But I was ready with my red hot poker. I lunged out with it, aiming at the source of the terrible smell.

> *In slow motion,* ***Absolon*** *charges across the stage to the booth.*

Absolon	(*Speaking in slow motion*) Ger-on-i-mo!

> *The poker makes contact with the bottom.* ***Nicholas*** *turns his head towards the audience, and opens his mouth in a silent scream. They all freeze.*

Miller	For Nicholas – time stopped still.
Absolon	(*Delighted*) And then he was flying through the air!
Nicholas	(*Leaping in the air*) Aaaaaaaaaaagh!
Absolon	(*Thrilled*) And then he landed on top of Alison!
Nicholas	(*Landing on top of Alison*) Aaagh!

Absolon	(*Ecstatic*) And then he screamed aloud again!
Nicholas	(*Clutching his bottom*) Aaaaagh! Help! Water! For God's sake – water!

Nicholas and Alison freeze.

Miller	Poor old John, you will remember, was upstairs asleep in his butter tub.
Nicholas	Water! Water!
John	(*Waking up in a panic*) Water? Water! The flood has come! Where's my axe?
Absolon	John cut the ropes holding the tub to the ceiling.

John mimes cutting the ropes.

Miller	But it wasn't the flood.
Absolon	And the butter tub didn't fall onto the water!

John looks at the audience startled.

Miller	The butter tub crashed…
John	Aaaaagh!

John mimes his long fall by using the three butter tubs as stages in his descent.

Absolon	… through the attic floor…
John	('*Falling' from his tub to the next one*) Aaaagh!
Miller	… through the ceiling beneath…
John	('*Falling' to the next tub*) Aaaagh!

During the next three speeches, John continues his 'fall' by moving through the side of the booth towards the stand-up bed.

Absolon	… through the next floor and ceiling…
John	Aaaagh!
Miller	… until he came to rest…

> *John ends up standing, spread-eagled, across the bed, on top of **Nicholas**, who is on top of **Alison**.*

Alison } **Nicholas** }	*(Painfully)* … on the bed!

> *There is chaos. **John**, **Nicholas** and **Alison** scream and struggle.*

Miller	Up leapt Alison and Nicholas…

> *Nicholas jumps off the bed. **Alison** comes out from between the covers. They call for help.*

Alison	Help!
Nicholas	Help!
Absolon	… and ran into the street!

> *Alison and **Nicholas** leave the booth and run downstage to the audience. **Nicholas** is still hopping about with pain. **Absolon** runs into the audience, stage right. **John** is left, sitting dazed, in the booth.*

Miller	All the neighbours came to find out what the trouble was!

> *There is further chaos as the **Alchemists** and other spare members of the cast, rush onto the stage. They bustle and jostle; arguing and questioning Nicholas, Alison, each other, and the audience. This should be improvised at the same time as, and in addition to, the dialogue that follows.*

Alison	Help! Call a doctor! Help! Water!
Nicholas	(*Still in agony and looking for Absolon*) Where is he? Where is he? I'll kill him!
Giovanni	What's going on?
Jocasta	What's all the screaming about?
Alison	The ceiling! The ceiling fell on me!

> *An actor wearing the same costume as Geoffrey has to swop places with the mannequin, which must be removed from the set. The following sequence, in which Nicholas pursues Absolon, is a good one to do it in, while the audience's attention is distracted from the stage.*

Nicholas	(*Spotting Absolon in the audience*) There he is! (*He points*)

> *The crowd fall silent and look where* **Nicholas** *is pointing.*

Nicholas	There he is, over there! Let me at him!
Amelia	(*Holding onto Nicholas*) He's gone mad!
Michelangelo	Hold him back!
Nicholas	(*Shouting to Absolon*) I'll get you! You wait! I'll skin you alive for this!
Jocasta	What'd he do?
Nicholas	(*Turning to Jocasta*) Ask him! Ask him!

> **Absolon** *quickly passes the poker to a member of the audience.*

Nicholas	Burned me with a red hot poker!
Absolon	Wasn't me!

Nicholas	Well, who else was it, then?
Absolon	(*Pointing to the audience member*) It was him/her!

*Everyone on stage starts to speak at once, arguing and commenting on this. Then **John** rises to his feet in the booth and shouts over them.*

| John | It was God! |

There is a sudden silence from everyone.

| Jocasta | You what? |
| John | God told me to sit in a butter barrel and wait for the flood – and then I fell through the ceiling onto the bed and found my wife, naked, with the student lodger! |

Everyone immediately roars with laughter.

| John | (*Coming down from the booth*) Clear off! Clear off the lot of you! |

*The crowd disperses, stifling laughter. **Michelangelo** exits stage right. **Absolon** makes his way quickly onto the stage. The cast of the Miller's Tale finish off their story by speaking directly to the audience.*

| Miller | And so the carpenter's wife got laid. |

John roars in anger.

Alison	Despite her husband's jealousy!
Nicholas	And Absolon has kissed her bottom eye!
Absolon	And Nicholas is blistered on his bum.
Cast	And God save all of us! This tale is done!

They all bow.

Finale

> *Michelangelo runs on from stage right.*

Michelangelo Stop! Stop! I heard something!

> *The other **Alchemists** stand up.*

Jocasta Me too!

Amelia Geoffrey!

> *The cast of the Miller's Tale and the **Alchemists** race to Geoffrey. They carry him to the downstage edge of the table but as they sit him down he suddenly comes back to life. As **Geoffrey** stands up, everyone on stage scatters.*

Geoffrey (*Furiously indignant*) Namoore of this, for Goddes dignitee!
Thou makest me so wery of thy verray lewednesse
That also wisely God my soule blesse
Myne eres aken of thy drasty speche!

Giovanni Geoffrey!

Michelangelo You're alive!

Amelia It's us!

Jocasta The Alchemists!

Geoffrey You villains! You owe me five hundred pounds!

Jocasta We gave you the elixir of eternal life!

Geoffrey You poisoned me! (*He looks around*) Is this not hell?
(*He examines the cast and the audience*) Are you not demons in hell? Am I not roasting in hellfire for writing those sinful Canterbury Tales, which even now I had to watch performed so badly by evil demons as a punishment for writing them! Am I not burning in hellfire?

Amelia No! You're on stage in... (*add name of place*)

Geoffrey	Am I? (*He is amazed*) Am I brought to life?
All	Yes!
Geoffrey	Let me see…

(*Remembering*) When April with his showers sweet
The drought of March has pierced to the root,
When the West Wind with its sweet breath
Has given life to every wood and field,
(*In his stride now*) – and when the young sun
Has run his half-course under Aries the Ram,
(*Triumphantly*) Then people long to go on pilgrimage!

*There are cheers and applause from everyone
as the whole cast crowd on stage. Everyone
joins in to sing the final song, in a medieval
style with a strong beat.*

Cast

It happened in that season on a day,
In Southwark at the Tabard as I lay,
All set to set out on my pilgrimage,
To Canterbury, to pay my deep homage

In fellowship, for pilgrims are we all – are we all!
In fellowship, for pilgrims are we all!

That night there came into that hostelry
Some nine and twenty in a company,
All kinds of folk that by adventure fall
In fellowship, for pilgrims were they all!

In fellowship for pilgrims are we all!
In fellowship for pilgrims are we all!
In fellowship for pilgrims are we all – are we all!
In fellowship for pilgrims are we all!

*Everyone bows. Accompanied by music, the
cast, led by* **Geoffrey**, *process off stage.*

Activities

About the Author   101
Chaucer's World   102
Chaucer's Pilgrims   104
Chaucer's Language   107
What the Adapter Says   110
Design Ideas   111

About the Author

Although Geoffrey Chaucer is considered to be the first great English poet, very little is known about his early life. It is thought that he was born in 1340 and was the son of John Chaucer, a prosperous wine merchant and tavern keeper.

In 1357, Chaucer became a page at Court and was soon serving in the household of King Edward III. In 1359, he fought in the French wars but was taken prisoner. He was ransomed (even the King gave sixteen pounds towards the ransom payment) and returned to England.

During the following years, Chaucer travelled abroad on the King's service (quite possibly as a spy). He visited Italy, Spain, Flanders, and France several times. During these visits he was introduced to Italian literature and he began his own writing career.

In 1374, Chaucer was made controller of Customs in the Port of London. He gave this post up in 1386 and began writing his best known work, **The Canterbury Tales**, a task that would occupy him for the rest of his life. Chaucer died in 1400 aged about sixty. He was buried in Westminster Abbey in the part that has become known as Poets' Corner.

Chaucer's World

Read

The world of Geoffrey Chaucer was very different from our modern world. He was born into a time of great upheaval and hardship. Death and illness were never very far away and life expectancy was a lot less than it is today. Social positions were rigidly defined. At the top of society was the king, followed by the nobility. The gentry, smaller landowners and merchants made up the middle classes, whilst at the bottom of society were the serfs who were 'owned' by the nobility.

Religion

The Catholic Church was a very important institution in medieval times. Everyone was expected to attend church from the king to the lowest peasant. The leader of the church was the Pope who lived in Rome. He had great power across Europe.

In England, there were hundreds of religious houses run by monks, friars and nuns. Although the majority of priests and nuns were good people, there were a number of religious hypocrites who would tell people to act in one way, and then behave differently themselves. In **The Canterbury Tales**, Chaucer is scathing about Church employees, like the Pardoner, who abuses the system by selling pardons (to those who want to pay a penance for their sins) to make money for his own ends.

Pilgrimages

Pilgrimages were an important part of medieval life. They were a combination of tourism, adventure and religious duty. By going on a pilgrimage, people believed that their sins could be forgiven, their illnesses cured and their souls saved.

The Canterbury pilgrimage was one of the great pilgrimages of medieval times. The other important pilgrimages were to Rome (home of the Pope), to Jerusalem, to the shrine of the Magi in Cologne, and to Santiago de Compostella in Spain. Pilgrims visited Canterbury to see the tomb of Saint Thomas à Becket, a former archbishop of Canterbury who was murdered in 1170 on the orders of King Henry II. Many miracles supposedly happened after his death and he was made into a saint in 1172. His shrine was placed in Canterbury Cathedral in 1220 and it soon attracted a large number of pilgrims, from all walks of society – kings, princes and ordinary people.

Such pilgrimages were difficult. Roads were poor and maps were rare. The journey to Canterbury from London would have taken three to four days. It is on such a journey to Canterbury that Chaucer sets his **Canterbury Tales**.

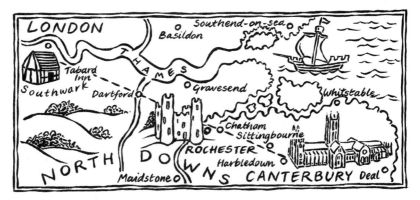

A map of the route taken by Chaucer's pilgrims from the Tabard Inn in Southwark to Canterbury Cathedral.

The Canterbury Tales

Read

Written from around 1386 onwards, **The Canterbury Tales** are made up of twenty-four stories told by a band of pilgrims, travelling from the Tabard Inn, Southwark in London to Thomas à Becket's tomb in Canterbury Cathedral. This is an ideal device for a series of stories. A cross-section of medieval society is represented in the tales from the high social ranking of the Knight down to the humble, lowly village Ploughman. There is also a range of different personalities as the gregarious Wife of Bath rubs shoulders with the shifty Pardoner. This structure allows Chaucer a variety of tales and many voices, with each tale matching the personality and interests of the pilgrim telling it.

Chaucer never completed **The Canterbury Tales**. He set himself the task of having all thirty pilgrims tell four tales each: two each on the way to Canterbury and two each on the way back. The teller of the best tale was to win a supper on their return to the Tabard Inn, paid for by the rest of the pilgrims. In the event, only twenty-four tales were started and not all of them were completed. Nevertheless, even as it stands, **The Canterbury Tales** remains one of the great works of world literature.

Write

Imagine that your class is going on a journey – this could be a visit to a stately home or a geography field trip – and you decide to tell stories to each other to pass the time.

1   As a class, decide where you are going.
2   Each person in the class should invent a character who is going on this trip and write a description of them.
3   Then, write a story that your character could tell. Remember, like Chaucer's stories, your tale has got to match the personality of the teller.
4   When you have finished, read your stories out and, as a class, decide who has won the supper at the Tabard Inn!

Chaucer's Pilgrims

The Prologue to Chaucer's **Canterbury Tales** contains a series of
wonderful descriptions about a variety of characters spanning the whole of
English society as it was in the Fourteenth century.

Read   1   Find a copy of Nevill Coghill's modern translation of **The Canterbury
Tales**. In small groups, read the descriptions of the following pilgrims as
they appear in The Prologue.
- The Knight
- The Wife of Bath
- The Miller
- The Pardoner

2   Write a brief description of each pilgrim, and try to answer the following
questions:
- What class of society do they come from – upper, middle, lower, etc.?
- What job do they do?
- What is their personality?
- What is Chaucer's view of them – does he appear to like them, or not?

3   Share your descriptions with the rest of the class.

4   Back in your groups, compare these descriptions with how the same
pilgrims are described and/or presented in Martin Riley's playscript:
- The Pardoner   (p.18 onwards)
- The Wife of Bath   (p.52 onwards)
- The Knight   (p.77)
- The Miller   (p.83 onwards)

Has Martin Riley been faithful to Chaucer's character descriptions?
If not, what has he changed?

Chaucer's Pilgrims, by William Blake

The Tales

In this playscript, Martin Riley chose to retell the tales told by the following pilgrims: the Pardoner, the Nun's Priest, the Wife of Bath, the Knight, and the Miller.

Research   1   Divide into small groups, then choose one of the tales (make sure they are all covered within the class). Each group has responsibility for collecting as much information as possible about their given tale.

This information must include a synopsis of the tale and some background research.

The synopsis should include the following pieces of information:
- who tells the tale
- a list of characters
- where it takes place
- what happens in the tale
- what the moral of the story is (if there is one).

The background research will help you to understand the context of the story. For each tale there are a number of topics to look at and some questions you should try and answer.

The Knight's Tale: a tale of romance and chivalry set in ancient times.

Research
- the hundred years war
- the crusades
- chivalry

Questions
- What was a knight's job?
- How did a knight dress?
- Where would a knight live?
- Why do you think the Knight chooses to tell this particular tale?

The Pardoner's Tale: a tale with a moral message, delivered by a crafty salesman!

Research
- religion in the Fourteenth century
- the Black Death
- relics and indulgences

Questions
- What was a pardoner's job?
- How was he different from priests and monks?
- What is the reaction of the other characters to the Pardoner?
- How do you think an audience would react to the Pardoner?
- Why do you think the Pardoner chooses to tell this particular tale?

The Wife of Bath's Tale: a traditional tale, told by the most out-going of Chaucer's pilgrims.

Research
- the role of women in medieval society
- chivalry
- pilgrimages

Questions
- Is the Wife of Bath a typical example of a woman in medieval Britain? If not, why not?
- How would she fit into medieval society?
- How does she compare to other women mentioned in this playscript?
- Do you think that the answer to the question: 'What is it that women most desire' is the correct one?
- Why do you think the Wife of Bath chooses to tell this particular tale?

The Nun's Priest's Tale: a typical fable – a story with a moral in which animals take on human characteristics.

Research
- nuns and monks in medieval times
- *Aesop's Fables*
- examples of other stories where animals take on human characteristics

Questions
- How did a nun's priest fit into medieval society?
- How does the Nun's Priest compare with the Pardoner?
- What is the moral of the tale he tells?
- Why do you think the Nun's Priest chooses to tell this particular tale?

The Miller's Tale: a bawdy story – one of the funniest of all the **Canterbury Tales.**

Research
- the working class in medieval society
- peasants and serfs
- trade in medieval England
- education in medieval times

Questions
- How did working conditions differ between tradespeople in the city and tradespeople in the countryside?
- What did a parish clerk's job involve?
- What were medieval schools and universities like?
- Why do you think that the Miller chooses to tell this particular tale?

2   When you have completed your research, each group has to deliver a report on its findings to the rest of the class in one or more of the following ways:
- as a talk
- as a written report
- as a wall display, using maps, pictures, charts, photocopies, and written captions
- as a radio programme (record this on a cassette tape)
- as a TV documentary (record this on a video tape).

Chaucer's Language

Read

Educated people in Chaucer's time could speak at least three languages: Latin, French and English. Chaucer wrote **The Canterbury Tales** in English, but it is not like the English we know today. Chaucer's English is hard to read at first, for several reasons:

- Some words are similar to modern English, but are spelt differently.
- Some words are very different or no longer exist.
- The word order is different to what we are used to (partly because Chaucer was writing poetry, but also because word order *was* different in the Fourteenth century).
- There was no agreement on how words should be spelled; Chaucer just wrote each word as it sounded when it was spoken (more or less as small children do as they are learning to write).

The Original Pardoner's Tale

Read Aloud and Brainstorm

The best way to get to grips with the original **Canterbury Tales** is to read them aloud. This is how the Pardoner begins his tale in Chaucer's version.

Thise riotoures thre of whiche I telle,
Long erst er **prime** rong of any belle
Were set her in a taverne for to drynke,
And as they sat, they herde a belle clynke
Biforn a cors, was caried to his grave.
That oon of hem gan callen to his knave:
'Go **bet**,' quod he, 'and axe redily
What cors is this that passeth here forby;
And look that thou reporte his name weel.'

prime *was the early morning service for monks. A bell was rung to call them to prayer*

bet: *quickly*

1 Read the lines around the class, or listen while they are read to you.
2 As a class, brainstorm the meaning of each line in modern English. If you don't know exactly what a word means, make a 'best guess'.
3 Some especially hard words are explained for you alongside the text. If you get really stuck on a word, you may have to look it up in a glossary like the one at the back of Oxford Student Texts, *General Prologue to the Canterbury Tales* by Geoffrey Chaucer.

Brainstorm and Write

Below are three speeches made by characters in The Pardoner's Tale: the boy, the taverner (innkeeper) and the riotour (hooligan).

1   Divide the class into four groups and allocate a section of the tale to each group.

2   Each group has to write out its character's speech in lively modern English. (The boy's speech is split into two because it's the longest.)

3   Here are some tips to help you in this task.

- Brainstorm your ideas amongst the group before deciding on what a line means and make rough notes.
- Don't get stuck for ages on something you don't understand – leave a blank and go on.
- When you write up your final translation into modern English, you will probably have to change the order of the words for some lines.

Group 1: the boy

'Sire,' quod this boy, 'it nedeth never-a-deel;
It was me toold er ye cam heer two houres.
He was, pardee, an old felawe of youres;
And sodeynley he was yslayn **to-nygyt**   **to-nygyt:** *ie last night*
Fordronke, as he sat on his bench upright.
There cam a privee theef men clepeth Deeth
That in this country al the peple sleeth,
And with his spere he smoot his herte atwo,
And wente his wey withouten wordes mo.

Group 2: the boy

'He hath a thousand slayn this pestilence.
And, Maister, er ye come in his presence,
Me thynketh that it were necessarie
For to be war of swich an adversarie.
Beth redy for to meete him everemoore;
This taughte me my dame; I sey namoore.'

Group 3: the taverner

'By seinte Marie!' seyde this taverner,
'The child seith sooth, for he hath slayn this yeer,
Henne over a mile, withinne a greet village,   **Henne over a mile:** *just a mile away, over there*
Bothe man and womman, child, and **hyne**, and page;   **hyne:** *servant*
I trow his habitacioun be there.
To been avysed greet wysdom it were,
Er that he dide a man a dishonour.'

Group 4: the riotour

'Ye, Goddes armes!' quod this riotour,
'Is it swich peril with hym for to meete?
I shal hym seke by wey and **eek** by strete,   **eek:** *also*
I make avow to Goddes **digne** bones!   **digne:** *holy*
Herkneth, felawes, we thre been al ones;
Lat ech of us holde up his hand til oother,
And ech of us bicomen otheres brother,
And we wol sleen this false traytour Deeth.
He shal be slayn, he that so manye sleeth,
By Goddes dignitee, er it be nyght!'

4   When you have completed your translation, read it out to the rest of the
    class.
5   Decide which group has best managed to combine the sense of the original
    with a lively modern translation.

Discuss   Compare your translation with the opening of The Pardoner's Tale in the
            play (pages 22–30), and discuss the following points:
            • Why do you think the play version includes the character Ambrosius,
              instead of the 'old felawe' (friend) of the rioters?
            • Why is this character played by a member of the audience?
            • What other differences are there between the way The Pardoner's Tale
              begins in the two versions? Can you suggest any reasons for these?

A panel from a stained glass window in Canterbury Cathedral in memory of the
many pilgrims who travelled to the shrine of St Thomas à Becket.

What the Adapter Says

This dramatization of **The Canterbury Tales** began over fifteen years ago as an improvised street performance based on The Pardoner's Tale, with me as the Pardoner and people plucked out of the audience to play the three medieval hooligans, the old man, the tree – even the treasure they found under its branches!

A few years later I decided to add more tales. I didn't want to keep changing into different pilgrims and, in a flash of inspiration, I decided to tell them all as a vulgar, fluffy-slippered, stripy-socked Yorkshire Victorian pantomime dame – with the fool's licence to cheek the audience! I called the show 'Dame Flossie Jollinickers Does Chaucer' and I've still got photographs of me in a wig, frock and bosoms to prove it.

This show was a great success and was performed, still without any written script, in schools, universities, pubs, and community centres with lots of audience participation. Flossie told the tales in modern English in a way that enabled the audience to recognize Chaucer's characters as people they might meet today. I wanted the stories to be as immediately accessible as they had been before they became 'medieval classics'.

Then came Alive & Kicking Theatre Co. who commissioned me to write an ensemble version for four actors to tour Europe and which has now been performed over 400 times, often to audiences whose first language is not English. Flossie had retired from the stage, so the four actors had to play all the pilgrims as well as most of the characters in the stories. Several parts, however, were still given to unsuspecting members of the public and there was plenty of participation, as when the knight, Sir Codsbrain, from The Wife of Bath's Tale interrogated the audience to find the answer to the question: 'What is it that women most desire?'

It was this 'fourhander' that formed the basis for this large-cast Oxford Playscript, so you'll find it easy enough to double up the characters if you're short of actors. I've also added an extra tale, The Knight's Tale, which is easy to remove if you wish to shorten the running time.

The important thing is to keep the performance fresh, lively, and fun with strong characterization, a strong physical style, plenty of pace, action and constant audience contact. It should still have the spirit of the street entertainment from which my adaptation sprang and the generous-hearted humanity and humour of Geoffrey Chaucer.

When you read the narrative poems of **The Canterbury Tales**, as I hope you will one day, you may be surprised to discover how close these dramatizations are to the originals, often where you least suspect it. As Geoffrey Chaucer himself said, 'My author will I follow if I can!'

Martin Riley

Design Ideas

Costumes

Discuss and Design

Would you choose to produce this play using elaborate costumes, or would you prefer to keep the costumes as simple as possible?

1 Divide the class into small groups, each of which will design costumes for a single tale or group of characters.

2 In your groups, discuss the costumes you will need for your characters. It may help to think about the following questions.
- What sort of costumes would a travelling theatre company carry?
- How big a company would you use to put on the play, and how would this affect costume changes?
- How could you quickly costume the members of the audience who become involved in the play?
- Do you need to make the 'animal' characters look like animals, or can they look like humans who behave like animals?

3 Then, produce some design sketches.

4 Finally, present your ideas to the rest of the class.

Masks

Discuss and Design

Masks provide a good way of adopting an instant character. Would you use masks for all the characters in the play, or only some? How would you decide? (Bear in mind that any mask will limit the actors' facial expressions, and will call for a different acting style which depends a lot more on body language. Full face masks will also make it difficult to hear the actors, and for this reason 'half-masks' that leave the mouth free are much better for scripted theatre.)

1 Split into small groups and talk about how you would use masks in a production of the play.

2 Design the masks that might be worn by three or four of the characters.

3 Present your designs to the rest of the class. If you have the time and resources, make the masks you have designed and see how well they work.

Music

Listen

Martin Riley's advice for the performance itself is to use live, improvised sound. But, if you wish to have music playing as the audience comes into the theatre, or during the interval; or if you just want to listen to some music of the Middle Ages to help you achieve the 'feel' of the style, you could try listening to:
- Telman Susato: *Dansereye 1551*
- Michael Praetorius: *Dances from Terpsichore*

These, and a wide range of fifteenth- and sixteenth-century dance music, are available on CD. Talk to your local library or record store; they will be able to help you.

Plays in this series include:

Across the Barricades
   Joan Lingard   adapted by David Ian Neville
                                ISBN 0 19 831272 5

The Bonny Pit Laddie
   Frederick Grice   adapted by David Spraggon Williams
                      with Frank Green
ISBN 0 19 831278 4

The Burston School Strike
   Roy Nevitt
ISBN 0 19 831274 1

The Canterbury Tales
   Geoffrey Chaucer   adapted by Martin Riley
ISBN 0 19 831293 8

Carrie's War
   Nina Bawden   adapted by Robert Staunton
ISBN 0 19 831295 4

The Demon Headmaster
   Gillian Cross   adapted by Adrian Flynn
ISBN 0 19 831270 9

Frankenstein
   Mary Shelley   adapted by Philip Pullman
ISBN 0 19 831267 9

Hot Cakes
   Adrian Flynn
ISBN 0 19 831273 3

Jane Eyre
   Charlotte Brontë   adapted by Steve Barlow and Steve Skidmore
ISBN 0 19 831296 2

Johnny and the Dead
   Terry Pratchett   adapted by Stephen Briggs
ISBN 0 19 831294 6

Paper Tigers
   Steve Barlow and Steve Skidmore
ISBN 0 19 831268 7

A Question of Courage
   Marjorie Darke   adapted by Bill Lucas and Brian Keaney
ISBN 0 19 831271 7

Smith
   Leon Garfield   adapted by Robert Staunton
ISBN 0 19 831297 0

A Tale of Two Cities
   Charles Dickens   adapted by Steve Barlow and Steve Skidmore
ISBN 0 19 831292 X

Tess of the D'Urbervilles
   Thomas Hardy   adapted by David Calcutt
ISBN 0 19 831439 6

The Turbulent Term of Tyke Tiler
   adapted from her own novel by Gene Kemp
ISBN 0 19 831269 5